Fashion Drawing in VOGUE

With 301 illustrations, 90 in color

Fashion Drawing in VOGUE

WILLIAM PACKER

Preface by David Hockney

 Thames and Hudson

To Clare and Charlotte,
Claudia and Katherine

Designed by Elizabeth Wickham

© 1983 The Condé Nast Publications Ltd, London

First published in paperback in the United States in 1989
by Thames and Hudson Inc., 500 Fifth Avenue,
New York, New York 10110
Reprinted 1997

Library of Congress Catalog Card Number 88-51325
ISBN 0-500-27528-9

Printed and bound in Singapore

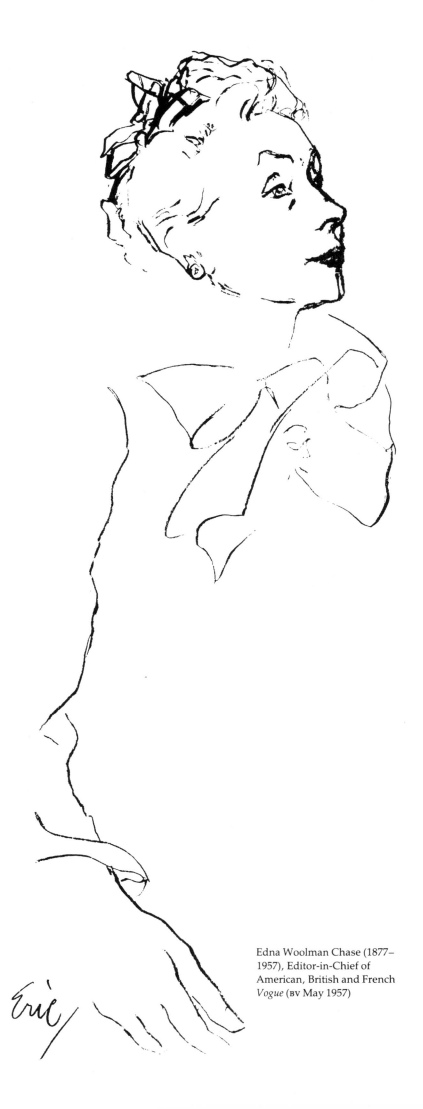

Edna Woolman Chase (1877–
1957), Editor-in-Chief of
American, British and French
Vogue (BV May 1957)

Contents

This is, before all else, a book of drawings, just drawings; and I think it is beautiful. I love books of drawings anyway, and what I like here is that they are drawings of a kind that is no longer familiar, and that we are not used to seeing collected in this way. They are marvellously fresh and alive. But even so, towards the end of the book we can see clear evidence of a decline, both in the skill of drawing itself, and in the use to which it is put. The artists who made those drawings in the twenties and thirties and forties could draw better than a lot of so-called serious artists working today – they could simply draw better: and it is particularly interesting that theirs was drawing done not for its own sake, but to be useful. It had a use. It was telling you all kinds of things – things about clothes, Paris, fashion, a whole way of life. The best drawings are never just blank faces but clearly carry the personality of the real figure, the live and active model.

It is easy to see what happens when people are not taught to draw – in fact it is visible everywhere else too, in one way or another, though perhaps rather harder to see. Certainly it is bound to be reflected in design, in the environment, in the way things are built, in the things we use and are forced to have around us. The serious study of looking, which is what drawing is, affects far more than we might casually think it does. Indeed it goes far beyond the limits of art itself, in the conventional sense, and is all the more serious for that, and should be treated more seriously by everyone. Even in a field as narrow and specialized as that of fashion, we can see the power drawing has to sharpen our eyes, and therefore the rest of our senses, to the world at large; and I would think that any reasonable and sensitive eye looking through this book would recognize this. And if there has been a decline, it is not at all wrong to point it out, even in this book, for it must help the future. The awareness of decline is the first and most necessary step towards stopping that decline. I think the point should be made over and over again.

Those artists were doing a specific job, the artist's job; and that too has now changed. Far fewer commissions are given than before: it seems not to occur to people that artists can have a job to do, a part to play. But we do not quite know which comes first. The editor of a famous Sunday newspaper once told me he had wanted to use artists, but was disappointed by those he saw and was put off. Perhaps he should have persevered with one or two and brought them on – most of the artists in this book began quietly before flourishing over many years. But it is a spiral, I suppose, with poor drawing discouraging its own use, and lack of encouragement depressing it further. Drawing is something that can be taught, after all, and I would have thought that exciting drawing would still be used if it were there.

Photography is not the answer, and anyway it has become very boring, repetitive and limited, especially in the fashion magazines. I cannot easily tell one cover from another – the girls the same, the lighting the same. Preparing the model, the make-up, the lights: it is all related to the theatre really, in a way that drawing never is. You can train yourself to observe and remember, to absorb and recreate, but the camera can only deal with what is in front of it at the time. Whether from memory and experience or from the model, the artist works in his own time, simplifying and transforming what he sees and knows into something of his own.

Nothing will change unless these things become clearer to people; and this book will help to achieve that in its way. I would like my criticisms to be taken in that spirit. The best of these artists were artists first and fashion artists second. They were simply taught to draw: and if any young artist is serious enough in wishing to follow them, he too will see that drawing is the right priority.

David Hockney

Introduction

A wider tradition and a particular discipline

Meidias, red-figure hydria, 5th century BC

Artists have always been moved to draw and to paint beautiful women. From the beautiful to the fashionable, and on to fashion itself, there are not big steps. The good, the great, the rich and the powerful have always sought to leave to posterity the image, if not quite of how they see themselves, most certainly of how they would wish to be remembered; and the fashionable gloss on the picture that art of any period paints is as old as painting itself. The great masters were never too proud to add, even to their most consciously important and ambitious work, all the cockades and ribbons, ruffles and furbelows that their patrons required as no more than their due. And it is evident that the likes of a Velázquez or a Veronese, a Rembrandt, Gainsborough, Ingres or Degas took the keenest notice of whatever their subjects chose to wear – or, in fashionable caprice or fantasy, rather wished to be thought to have worn. Even the more private work – the immediate and perfunctory note hastily registered within the artist's sketchbook, the more elaborate and considered preparatory study, or the personal record of friend or family – confirms that artists have always had a general visual interest in the clothes a subject wears, in why or how they are worn, and in what they say of his or her place in the world.

The evidence is everywhere, in every age; from the Greek vase painter, with the delicate touch and fall of the diaphanous skirt across a thigh, to Watteau under the trees of Versailles, and the rustle and fold of silk and brocade upon the grass. We feel with our own eyes, with the direct *frisson* of a common experience and understanding, the young man's velvet cap, that Holbein so deftly describes, and the cold fall of the jewels at the Queen's throat. A hundred years later, and again we readily share in Hollar's careful enjoyment of his lady's long kid gloves, and her fur muffs and tippets. And then, later, there is the rich fall of silk at the waist of Ter Borch's courtesan, Gainsborough's lace, and the rough-and-tumble of Rowlandson petticoats. Degas's young dancing girls, stretching and pointing, get ready in the wings; Toulouse-Lautrec's rush stridently onstage.

Society in all its aspects has always been freely available to the artist as primary reference and material. Today, however, it seems that the happy conspiracy of natural vanity with creative energy and vision has somehow failed. Portraiture has suddenly become a self-conscious profession. The passing domestic comedy of manners is no longer the material of ambitious attention. It is left to the sophisticated mechanisms of photography to commit current dreams and vanities, styles and manners to posterity. But the artist cannot have changed in potential, for human nature is much as it was, and the eye is as likely as ever to be caught by the swing of a hip or the chance turn of a head and the fall of hair across the face. It seems that we have become the prisoners of our prejudices and expectations, and, taking the supposed answer as our excuse, would scarcely dream of asking an artist of independent reputation to paint or draw anything to do with fashion, for example, or indeed with any other special study. This is the age of the specialist, and it is believed that one must be bred to one's discipline: the artist, not having had cause to extend himself or stray into another field, is not asked in because he has not himself come forward. To see what is lost by such narrowness, it is necessary only to look back across a generation to a time when even the most distinguished and secure of artists might be set on his mettle by being asked, as it were, to step across. That is not to say that artists of the first rank are invariably fashion illustrators *manqués*. However, artists, if approached, will accept the commissions which interest them, and, if they need the money, even some which do not. All that is needed is a patron with the imagination to see the possibilities in such an enterprise and the courage to effect the connection.

Vogue, for the greater part of a distinguished existence, protagonist for more than seventy years in its special, self-set field of fashion and the civilized life, did just that, using artists straightforwardly for whatever they had to offer in terms

Hans Holbein, *Cecily Heron*, 1526–28

Wenceslaus Hollar, *Muffs and Lace*, 1647

9

of particular style and vision. The principal defining condition was only a demonstrable practical effectiveness, either in describing the close and characterizing details of the current mode, or in conveying that more general, encompassing and equally characteristic aura of refinement, elegance and chic. If the two approaches could somehow be combined, so much the better.

From 1909, when Condé Nast took over *Vogue*, the magazine's record of engagement with current developments in modern art, even if it amounted at times to little more than curiosity, was in general much better than might have been expected. Reviews and feature articles were regular items, and distinguished guests would appear occasionally within the editorial pages as contributors. But all this was bonus to the underlying policy, unstated and assumed as it was, that the graphic arts should hold a useful and rightful place in the natural scheme of things. Young, promising and interested artists were thus given the chance to prove themselves. Many of them turned out to be ordinary enough, competent draughtsmen supplying usable material reliably and in quantity; but even they, should they strike form, were given the opportunity to test and extend themselves, growing in confidence and practice over the months and years. Most of *Vogue*'s stars proved themselves in just this way, over an extended period, and so grew into the privileged freedom to do with the fashion what they could, or would, so long as the fashion itself was in essence described.

Sustained support, if at times dispensed somewhat arbitrarily, was the generous stimulant. Consequently the abundance of material thereby procured for *Vogue* over many years, even without reference to comparative and supplementary sources, is almost beyond collation and assimilation. This collective contribution – sophisticated, openly ambitious or experimental perhaps in the individual case, or orthodox, discreet, modest, even obscure – was the decisive influence upon the physical appearance of the magazine. It is easy to acknowledge the substantial effect upon *Vogue* of the work of its more conspicuous and celebrated illustrators, Eric and Willaumez, Benito and Mourgue, Bouché and Bérard; but even the drawings, the marginal *croquis* and vignettes supplied by minor, perhaps anonymous artists, often point the mood and spirit of the particular moment with a poignancy which photographs could never match. There is no more potent agent of recall than the illustrated magazine which, designed only to catch the passing moment on the wing, thus unselfconsciously, almost absently, stores it away to mature as it may. And where it is the artist who supplies its images, the substance is more particular, more personal, more piquant; for he or she cannot just accept, but must absorb and process it all, through the senses and imagination, and every mark becomes a kind of declaration.

This book celebrates that collective achievement of many decades. Perhaps it is not yet too late to call into question the absolute sway of the photograph,

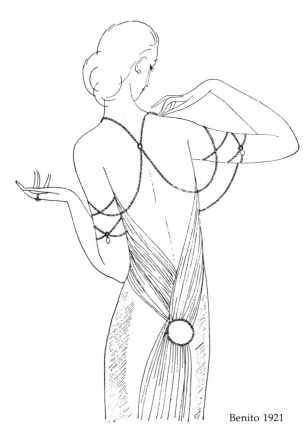

Benito 1921

powerful and evocative though it undoubtedly is, and great artists though so many of *Vogue*'s photographers were and are. The drawn or painted image may be at least as effective, in describing all we need to know of any particular technicality or detail; and from the right pen it is infinitely more adaptable and subtle in its evocation of style and gesture. The camera, with its beady single eye and all its tricks and chemicals, rarely gets any nearer to the truth than the hand with its pencils, line and colour.

Marty 1922

It is not, of course, a competition. Photographs were always deployed comfortably in harness with drawings, their natural complement. This is the story of those drawings as used by *Vogue* in these years: from Nast's earliest days, when the cover was the principal graphic feature of the magazine and there was a mass of comparatively undistinguished material inside, through the days of graphic maturity and excellence, to the present, when the appearance of a drawing at all is something of a treat.

In human affairs of every kind, all periods, even those apparently most settled and secure, are times of transition, of shifting states, attitudes and interests. It is natural, when we look back, to try to recognize a pattern; but nothing can be quite as simple or as clear as we might wish, and it is important not to attach too much significance to those dates, events, conspicuous individuals, that have been singled out perforce to mark each period. No thunderbolt ever comes out of a clear sky; and though the artist may seem to set himself positively against the times, he remains inescapably of them and must tacitly accept them. He must take things as they come, working and waiting for the opportunities of exposure, criticism, patronage and support. In the arts expression is never truly spontaneous, born of the moment out of nothing, and achievement comes long and hard. Just when did the work, upon which the epoch would appear to turn, first take effect: at conception perhaps, or completion, or publication, or long afterwards, even decades later? Such retrospective acknowledgment may be significant only to those who live to see it.

This survey of the editorial use of drawing by *Vogue* begins in the early twenties with a decidedly variegated bag of contributors, both gifted and mundane, and continues to the present, following first the rise to a spirited and varied excellence of performance and then the decline to the withdrawal of consistent editorial support in the early sixties and on to the present policy of sporadic and spontaneous commissions.

It is reasonable, therefore, to concentrate upon the middle period, which embraces the greater achievement, but to define that period as beginning in the late twenties may well occasion a certain surprise. There have, after all, been major critical revivals and reassessments in recent years, first of Art Nouveau, and then of the Art Deco that grew out and away from it. Both movements had been more than adequately monitored by *Vogue*, and many of the covers of the magazine in Nast's first twenty years still stand among their more spectacular

George Plank 1927

and decorative popular examples. With the monopoly of those drawn and painted covers unbroken by the photograph until the summer of 1932, the received wisdom is that *Vogue*'s golden age of illustration must surely have been a little earlier.

This is the story, however, not of the cover, but of what was used within the editorial body of the magazine. It is not to demean the graphic gifts and achievements of the stars who shone through those earlier times and phases, so publicly upon the bookstall counter with *Vogue* itself as yet unopened, to point the distinction. Condé Nast may have valued the artists he brought to *Vogue* from the pages of *La Gazette du Bon Ton* – Georges Lepape, André Marty, Pierre Brissaud, Edouard Benito and their colleagues – and relished the decorative fantasies of George Plank and Helen Dryden; but only on the cover was any one of them allowed fuller scope. It was only with the access of colour reproduction for editorial use, at the opening of the thirties, which coincided with Eric's own first cover and his first more tentative colour plates inside, that illustrators came into their own within the magazine. By then most of that earlier generation had had their day. *Vogue* entered its most adventurous period, not only in illustration, but in layout and design, at just the time when those artists who had been among its most radical spirits appear to have fallen away.

Most of the *Gazette* group had been young artists, fresh from the Ecole des Beaux-Arts in the Paris of those years just before the First World War, a city highly charged with creative energy, excitement and the stimulation of positive achievement and advance. In perhaps the single most important period in the history of modern art, it was the Paris of Picasso and Braque deep in their Cubist adventure, of Fauvism and emergent Expressionism, of Kandinsky's first Expressionist abstractions, of Mondrian's early reductive geometries, of Brancusi's infinitely refined simplicity, of Matisse at full stretch, of Léger, Bourdelle, Modigliani, Laurens and Duchamp. It was the Paris of young Stravinsky and, most especially, of Diaghilev and his *Ballets Russes*, set and dressed by Léon Bakst with a wonderfully extravagant and influential exoticism.

No art world, not even in the greatest of modern capitals, can ever be much more than a kind of village of the mind, that anyone may choose to enter, given the will and a little luck; and the bounds of the several parishes are never set, but always moving and blurring against each other. There was in Paris at that time the most natural intercourse between poet and painter, composer, decorator, designer, couturier. Paul Iribe knew Jean Cocteau, who knew . . . whom did he not know? It is unthinkable that the *Gazette* group of alert, ambitious and committed young men should not have felt positively involved in the great things being done so close at hand.

But influences must also be assimilated, perhaps deflected, to serve practical ends, as they become absorbed into the common stock of visual devices. Like water coming through the roof, they may reveal themselves with a certain obvious directness, but they are quite as likely to follow a more devious path, turning up who knows when, or where, or having picked up what along the way. Thus the elegant elongations of Matisse, Modigliani and Bourdelle were not slow to affect contemporary Parisian graphic design and illustration. The heady atmosphere of the *Ballets Russes* lay across Parisian couture, Paul Poiret especially, and since much of that was what the artists of the *Gazette* described, it, too, was added to the brew.

The graphic and decorative possibilities of Cubism, on the other hand, and a little later of Constructivism, the Bauhaus and De Stijl, took longer to reveal themselves. Eventually they did, if at a certain remove, when informing the bobs and shingles, the straight lines, the clean tubes and spheres of the fashion of the later twenties and equivalent qualities in the other disciplines of applied design – architectural, industrial, domestic and graphic.

Expressionism took even longer to declare itself, possibly because the tighter conventions in the first place of Art Nouveau and then of Art Deco had exploited its peculiar properties, the freely cursive and expressive line fixed into the swirls and arabesques of the one, and the bold, directly stated and exuberant colour generously indulged by the other. Again it is curious that the Fauve simplicities and directness of Van Dongen or Matisse should begin to register themselves in

Mario Simon 1922

the pages of *Vogue* at just the point, as the twenties turn to the thirties, when the next generation is taking over. That the artists of the thirties, such as Eric, Willaumez and Grafstrom, should be a shade more revisionist still, consciously looking further back to Toulouse-Lautrec and Degas, only compounds the curiosity.

Modern art is always with us, and as the thirties move on, so in *Vogue* it becomes the turn of Surrealism to move from the coteries of the avant-garde into the public domain, just as Cubism had done that little time before. Surrealism became direct with the work of De Chirico, Dalí and Pierre Roy, and the photography of Cecil Beaton besides, and indirect but none the less influential in the Expressionist romanticism of Christian Bérard, his cocktail so generously spiked with the Surreal.

And so the story, which is the substance of this book, continues, *Vogue* changing subtly as its artists change with the times. The artists are celebrated as they celebrated their subject, the passing fashion. Asked to do a particular job, they regularly produced material that transcended mere documentation, their drawings no less considerable, no less fine art, for being so eminently practical, decorative, useful.

The tradition in which they worked was in part the tradition of the old fashion plate of the previous two hundred years, the work of competent and frequently anonymous journeymen-artists for the penny sheets and portfolios of the print-houses, and in part the higher, more ambitious tradition of personal observation, record and expression. This tradition was in no sense in decline until a surprisingly late date; it was not killed off at last by the camera; it might not even yet be dead, though it has been moribund these twenty years. The use of good drawing as an obvious, effective and distinctive means of particular description, in practice no less selective than a photograph, and always as pointed and informative as may be necessary, fell victim not to competition, not to any failure in the supply of artists, but to the failure of an editorial habit of mind. A regular practice would suggest an increasing knowledge of the material, besides a natural expertise; but with no artists in regular commission there can appear to be none to ask, and so the editorial prejudice feeds itself. It is obvious in these pages what can and might be done should it occur to anyone to ask capable artists – who, like modern art itself, are still here – to supply the deficiency.

Vogue admitted as much to itself from time to time, in its own way. During the years just after the Second World War, when the editors could hardly imagine the magazine without a regular and honoured place for its chosen artists, certain remarks were published about Eric, its greatest star. 'Eric', the magazine stated in 1946, 'makes fashion move and live on the pages of *Vogue* – makes the women move within the clothes he draws.' Three years later, a long article to mark an exhibition in New York of all aspects of his work was more specific: 'He draws only what he sees. But his genius is in seeing the essential and infusing it with

Eric 1929

Eric 1946 >

14

life. In his fashion drawings, the significant detail is stressed – the notched collar, the hem-deep panel, the gold-linked belt – those elements that give distinction. His drawings are so true that they tend to magnify anything that is phony. . . . His drawings are even more true than photographs, for by selectivity and discrimination he lays bare the essential.'

Most succinct of all was this sentence from its obituary notice of 1958: 'To the Paris couture an Eric drawing was the most desired of representations for their designs.'

ROCOCO

John Ward may have been concerned only with what he had been asked to describe – the London spring collections of 1949 (here Victor Stiebel's high shawl-collared evening dress in grey brocade); but the nostalgia of that mode itself for an ampler Rococo elegance and luxury is unmistakable, and it is hard not to read into the artist's own page of studies a conscious and delicate tribute to the master of that hedonistic age, Jean-Antoine Watteau. And if the *fête galante* has moved indoors, the gentle rustle of silk across the floor is still the same, and the catch of the skirt behind, the swell and fall of material about the hip, and the quick, stolen glance aside.

Eric 1947

16

IMPRESSIONISM

From Mary Cassatt, seen in the Louvre by her friend Degas (lower left), to René Bouché's equally parasoled young lady (right, 1948) is nearly seventy years, but no great step, with Helleu's Edwardian élégante (left), and Helen Dryden's mid-twenties flapper, furred and cloched (above left), to mark the way; but quite where Impressionism, so certain and familiar an epithet, fades into Expressionism is not altogether clear. As with all of Art's Isms, as with the Cheshire Cat, the more we look, the more the substance seems to dissolve away, leaving only the grin. But the word Impressionism serves well enough, the moving image caught on the wing, the suggestion made with rapid, knowing delicacy.

Tom Keogh (left, 1948) and Marcel Vertès (bottom, 1953), join René Gruau (right, 1949), who remains today the grand survivor among fashion illustrators, and even the occasional ornament still of French *Vogue*. Together they stand for the last confident, ebullient high style of *Vogue* as an illustrated magazine, all swish and line and unapologetic glamour. But modern as they are, and for all the contemporary flair and elegance that they display, they yet look back to a slighter older, larger graphic tradition in which they still hold a place. In particular they look back to Toulouse-Lautrec (below) and the infectious graphic freedoms of the nineties, Montmartre and the Moulin Rouge. And there is, too, a hint of the disciplined simplicities of the Japanese.

THE JAPANESE PRINT AND ART NOUVEAU

No influence, in art or fashion, can ever be entirely self-contained. The masters of the Japanese wood-block, unselfconsciously serving their enclosed domestic world, had more effect in the West than they could ever have dreamed of, and on all manner of artists. Here it is Art Nouveau, and Aubrey Beardsley (left) who openly acknowledges his graphic debt; and later Foujita, in *Vogue* itself (below left, 1931), with all Parisian sophistication at his fingers' ends, who turns again so elegantly to his cultural roots, the past reflected in the glass of the present. And Helen Dryden, too (right, 1923), who for all her wayward decorative instinct, never quite forgets those Eastern tricks, devices and refinements: 'the costume ball . . . unmasks the sobriety of conventional citizens and proves that the Colonel's lady and Judy O'Grady are fantastic and romantic creatures . . . *Vogue*, ever an exponent of the picturesque, offers charming designs by Miss Helen Dryden as its contribution to the success of such an occasion.'

EXPRESSIONISM

Expressionism can be many things, and the fierce and colourful directness that earned the Fauves their name of Wild Beasts should not blind us to the more decorative and domestic, even romantic Expressionism that followed, as attitudes and interests, even of those self-same artists, broadened, softened, ramified. The quiet, bourgeois, private preoccupations of Henri Matisse (left) belie the painter's graphic nerve, confidence and sophistication. Kees van Dongen (below left, 1926) brings to the softness of Cheney Silks a Fauvist bite: 'The luxury of line, the piquancy of striking pattern, may be expressed with equal felicity and allurement in painting and in silk.' *Vogue*'s own artists, Christian Bérard (below, 1937) and Carl Erickson (right, 1932), also serve commissioned and public ends, but the Fauve lesson is clearly not lost on them. Eric's, indeed, is as magnificent a statement of the Cover as any in the canon.

VOGUE

SUMMER ENTERTAINING
OLDER WOMEN'S FASHIONS

SURREALISM

Surrealism: the most accessible, literary, witty and gleefully outrageous of all the avant-garde movements of modern art. Its roots are deep, and infinitely ramified, running back through Symbolism and Romanticism and Gothic fantasy; but more immediately they lie with the desperate nihilism of Dada, laced with the introspective indulgences of Freudian psychology, freed technically by collage and experimental photography. Even if these other schools and disciplines may now bear the deeper analysis, in the later twenties and beyond, it was Surrealism, in all its deceptive maturity, that seemed the most obviously significant. *Vogue* took to it whole-heartedly, exploiting it, indulging it and even transforming it to bring out an unlooked-for element of decorative and poetic romanticism, elegant and seductive. Here are Dalí (left: American *Vogue*, 1949), Coltellacci (right: French *Vogue*, 1948), de Chirico (above right: American *Vogue*, 1937), and Benito (below right: American *Vogue*, 1939). Surrealism for *Vogue* was indeed modern art, and it influenced the magazine directly and profoundly, not only in the work of its illustrators but in that of its photographers and art editors.

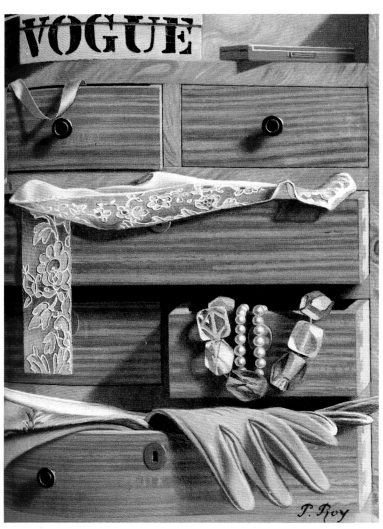

THE COVER AND MODERN ART

A cover is at once proclamation of identity and practical advertisement. For more than forty years, *Vogue* covers were characterized more by adventure and sophistication than by consistency. First Salvador Dalí (here on American *Vogue*, 1939) in the improbable desert of his dreams, adapting to the opportunity but conceding nothing: 'flowers for the beauty of women, a skipping figure for the remembrance of childhood, a skeleton ship for the sadness of things past'. Then Pierre Roy (British *Vogue*, 1938), quieter, more metaphysical than surrealist, his drawer yet to be opened, like *Vogue* itself. And Benito (British *Vogue*, 1929) looking straight at Modigliani (above) and the high experimental art of nearly twenty years before.

COLLAGE

Collage, the technique of bringing together disparate and extraneous elements within a single design, was first exploited by the Cubists: and here it is in Andy Warhol's Jubilee Year image of Queen Elizabeth II (far left, 1977). Richard Hamilton's *Fashion Plate Study* appeared in British *Vogue* in 1970 to mark his retrospective at the Tate Gallery (left), and the same year Antonio used collage in a real fashion plate (below): 'Wear the layers, the knickers and the languid silk dresses like this, and you're well away.'

1923-1934

*Art Deco and the artists of
the Gazette du Bon Ton
Fashion illustration and the
modern movement in art*

A CONTINUING TRADITION

It would be wrong to say that artists can
no longer deal with the woman and the
clothes she wears as their subject, or even
that their interest has faded. But nothing
can be done if the opportunity is lacking.
David Hockney is a conspicuously gifted
draughtsman, even pre-eminent in his
generation, and his unaffected studies of
his friends, of Celia Birtwell in particular,
demonstrate both his personal powers
and his sound, orthodox, technical base.
This lovely drawing, which British *Vogue*
took the opportunity to publish in 1973,
shows with a poignant clarity what can
be done.

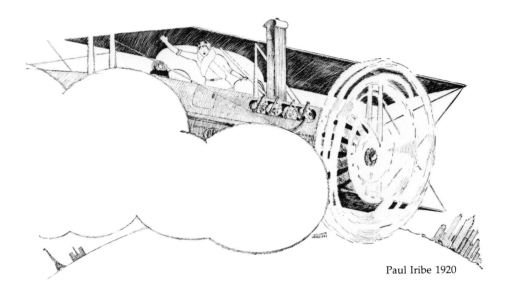

Paul Iribe 1920

With the New Year of 1923, *Vogue* was celebrating its first thirty years. Its three editions, British (established in 1916), French (1920) and, of course, the parent American edition, made up a well-established and truly international enterprise. But the *Vogue* that rode so high bore scant relation to the languishing parish journal of American east coast society that Condé Nast had taken over in 1909. He transformed it, and long before the First World War a magazine came into being that in its physical character and disposition, in its editorial scope, assumptions and interests, was the *Vogue* we know today.

This was a remarkable, even revolutionary proprietorial coup, as imaginative as it was ambitious. The formula he devised, a potent mixture of high fashion, high society, the arts, social advice dressed up as gentle satire, and gossip and snobbery unabashed, proved immediately and lastingly successful. The trick was simple: to appeal both to society itself, whose self-importance it continued generously to indulge, and to that wider, newer public, the massed, aspiring middle classes upon whom, in an advertiser's age, its circulation and thus its life depended.

For *Vogue*, as for any successful and lasting publication, a happy condition of permanent change is an essential characteristic. *Plus ça change*; Nast's initial transformation was worked within a year or two, and *Vogue* in 1923, in its physical appearance and editorial policies alike, was still manifestly *la même chose*. In 1923 it was modifying itself as ever, and was about to experience a quite considerable speeding up of that process. Poised, too, on the edge of change were all the artists who had collectively determined *Vogue*'s visual character.

Some had been with Nast almost from the beginning, others joined along the way; and many were now comfortably established, if not as senior, at least as regular and recognized, contributors. Some remain shadowy, peripheral figures, forever obscure behind an uncrackable monogram, illegible signature or, too often, no signature at all. Some who were consistent ornaments to *Vogue* remain tantalizingly mere names. A few were well known in their time, and interest in them has lasted or revived; only a very few were ever to stand as celebrities in *Vogue*'s own eyes, the subject of the pointed byline and the personal feature article. But sometimes an item did appear here, a snippet of information there, to thin the mist a little. Early in 1923 it occurred to *Vogue* that one small way to mark that thirtieth birthday would be to devote four pages to a parade of its current artist contributors.

The piece takes the character of an informal questionnaire enlivened by personal photographs and, in some cases, the reproduction of an artist's actual response, handwritten, doodled upon and otherwise enhanced; and though too little is still learned about any one of them – their modest snapshots affording us a bare glimpse of identity – for once something can at least be sensed of *Vogue*'s own attitudes and priorities.

First there are *Vogue*'s American artists posted in Paris, five of them, and two in London, and eleven more in New York; and then at last, and with rather a splash, come the eight French artists on *Vogue*'s accredited list, all of whom can only be assumed to be still in Paris at that time: Georges Lepape, Mario Simon, Charles Martin, Pierre Mourgue, Bernard Boutet de Monvel, Pierre Brissaud, André Marty and the Spaniard, Eduardo (Edouard) García Benito; George Barbier and Paul Iribe may be added to this little group, for their work had until recently been appearing intermittently in the magazine. Their association with *Vogue* is a little history in itself.

In 1908 Paul Poiret, the most modern-minded and adventurous of Parisian couturiers, had the bright idea to publicize himself by means of a slim and elegant volume in a strictly limited edition, fastidiously illustrated by Paul Iribe. So successful was *Les Robes de Paul Poiret* that three years later he repeated the exercise with *Les Choses de Paul Poiret*, illustrated by Georges Lepape. And the point was well made that the field of haute couture was wide open to the artist-illustrator, to the mutual advantage of all concerned. In 1911 Lucien Vogel and Michel de Brunhoff founded *La Gazette du Bon Ton*, an exquisitely precious publication that was to have, in its short, interrupted and uneven career, an influence quite disproportionate to its circulation. Boutet, Brissaud, Barbier, Lepape, Marty, Martin and Iribe – young, fashionable, elegant, talented – were soon buzzing around Vogel's decidedly special hive, and flitting and sipping in the Parisian clover like the natural worker-drones they were.

Condé Nast, of course, was soon very much aware of the *Gazette* and its artists; and indeed occasionally published them himself. When the First World War forced Vogel to suspend publication, Nast was quick to take them on more regularly, and even to give one or two of them (Lepape especially) the particular prominence of the cover. The *Gazette* returned in 1920, its stable augmented by such younger artists as Benito and Mourgue; in 1921 Nast bought it up, and he continued with it until 1925, when he closed it for good. This makes it all the

Bernard Boutet de Monvel 1922

George Barbier 1919

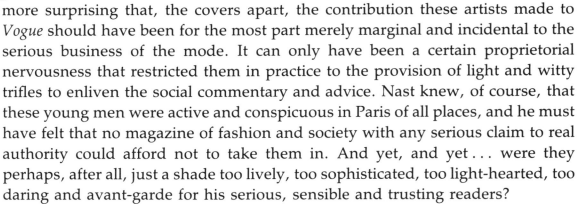

Pierre Brissaud, Lepape, Marty 1922

Pierre Brissaud 1923

Marty 1923

more surprising that, the covers apart, the contribution these artists made to *Vogue* should have been for the most part merely marginal and incidental to the serious business of the mode. It can only have been a certain proprietorial nervousness that restricted them in practice to the provision of light and witty trifles to enliven the social commentary and advice. Nast knew, of course, that these young men were active and conspicuous in Paris of all places, and he must have felt that no magazine of fashion and society with any serious claim to real authority could afford not to take them in. And yet, and yet... were they perhaps, after all, just a shade too lively, too sophisticated, too light-hearted, too daring and avant-garde for his serious, sensible and trusting readers?

If Modern Art is still hard for so many *soi-disant* educated people to take, how much harder it was in those early twenties, a mere ten years after that great period before the war, with the storm of innovation and experiment apparently by no means over. And these young men had seen it all, had been in the thick of it, and probably still were. Nast would always claim for *Vogue* 'the desire to promote all that is new in art (so long as it is inherently good and has the intangible quality of chic that characterizes all the material in the magazine)'. But he was never quite able to see that the work of his artists of the *Gazette* was shot through with just those qualities.

In the summer of 1922, in a sudden access of editorial confidence or change of heart, the *Gazette* troupe were thrust self-consciously to the centre of *Vogue*'s stage for a brief spell. *Vogue* announced to the ever attentive reader 'The True History and Exploits of Six Parisiennes, Their Manners and Their Modes, Their Foibles and the Fables They Tell, Set Down Each Month for VOGUE by the Artists of Their Choice.' The scheme was simple enough: these pretty young things, each with her artist in tow, were to appear in almost every issue, 'as one might meet at the house of a friend some young woman... who charms and wins a cordial admiration by her way of dressing, by some quality of her personality'.

Brissaud was allotted Sophie, elegant, cultivated, country-loving and devoted to Octave, her parrot; Marty to Sylvie, worldly, sophisticated, discreet and married, with a Siamese cat called Pouti; Charles Martin in the enthusiastic, precious Toinon and her goldfish, Anatole; Mario Simon to young Rosine, the cynosure of drawing-room and restaurant, who has twin parrakeets called Anis and Pistache; Lepape to the gay, romantic and hedonistic Françoise, with only her white elephant charm for pet; and Benito was assigned to high-born Palmyre, with her mother, Mme Toujours-en-retard, her godmother, Mme Comme-il-faut, her old friend, M. Tout-le-monde, and Youyou, her pekinese.

Charles Martin 1923

Charming, artificial, clever and diverting it all undoubtedly was, but clearly impossible to sustain; and indeed the True History and Exploits did not last long, slipping quietly out of mind within a year. But in that New Year of 1923, the elegant sextet were still very much about, so much so that *Vogue*'s anniversary celebration, a Prize Competition with models from the great Paris houses to be won, was cast around their daily social habits. What is more, colour reproduction was for once available within the editorial body of the magazine, a treat hardly to be repeated, certainly not to become commonplace, for nearly ten years. And so, with a splash of colour beautifully disposed, *Vogue* at the very start of this survey is to be found looking both ways at once.

The whole feel of the magazine in 1923 remains very much as it has been for ten years or more: the same general layout and design, the heavy borders to the pictures, the generous margins. But now it is just beginning to be accepted that the larger, bolder illustration, rather than remaining incidental and occasional, should have a regular and prominent place as the focus of attention, the source of positive and useful information.

Georges Lepape therefore sets off this survey with a splash of rich and subtle colour, his Françoise resplendent in her box at the opera; and Benito, Simon, Marty and Brissaud command its first few pages. But theirs is a deceptive pre-eminence, and short-lived. For *Vogue* remains as essentially American as ever,

Mario Simon 1923

Mario Simon, Benito, Charles Martin 1922

Benito 1924

and these charming, knowing, conspicuously clever and exquisitely daring young men are perhaps, after all, just a shade too mannered, distracting, foreign. Too soon they are back to their marginalia, to their heads and tails, to Beauty, Health, Travel and the Good Life; and the opportunity is gone.

Even in 1923, however, most of these artists were far from excessive in what they did, and as the twenties wore on their work grew ever quieter and, indeed, more straightforward. Only Benito remained openly experimental and provocative, unpredictable, responding at times chameleon-like to whatever his colleagues of the day were doing. He lasted longer with the magazine, and was employed more variously, than any of the others; and when a more consciously adventurous spirit returned a few years later with the high Surrealism of the thirties, he alone remained to enjoy it.

Though the work of these artists was not exploited fully within its pages, the cover of *Vogue* was made almost their preserve for ten years and more, with Benito, who was given *carte blanche* to simplify, abstract and decorate his fashionable graphic ideal, and Lepape the dominant presences until the middle thirties. Marty, Brissaud and, later on, Pierre Mourgue, all contributed consummately stylish, memorable and effective solutions to this highly specialized and exposed commission.

In this, as in all aspects of their work, a guiding principle remained the placing of fashion, specific or ideal, and all the trappings and circumstances of the civilized life, within a pleasurable and diverting context, rounded off by style

Pierre Brissaud 1923

and wit, elegance and chic. It would seem that nothing could be more generally sympathetic to *Vogue*'s own principles and disposition in that time, but it was left to the American illustrators, rivals and colleagues, to take on the responsibility for illustrating fashion. They effectively command the pages of *Vogue* throughout this early period, even at the very moment of that apparent Parisian ascendancy. Yet these Americans themselves were not insensitive or impervious to French example.

Condé Nast had acted upon his shrewd assessment of a domestic readership, and if he had sought to broaden its cultural and social horizons somewhat, crediting it with a genuine and sophisticated cosmopolitan curiosity, he remained in no doubt that he could only take it so far, and so fast. The expansion to British and French editions notwithstanding, there was never any question that the American was the senior edition and that its interests were paramount.

The ship was tightly run in those early years. British and American *Vogue* offered two issues a month (variously extended at times to twenty-six issues a year), and though they were never exactly in step, they shared editorial material to a remarkable extent, the fashion element often almost entirely. A certain latitude was allowed in matters of national usage and particular interest. The graphic material and the layouts were sometimes modified or rearranged, the emphasis shifted slightly. But that was all. Except for the obvious differences celebrated in the social pages, and the local requirements of advertising, over any several months, as copy, photographs and drawings made their way to and fro across the Atlantic, the British and American editions were palpably the same *Vogue*.

When things were not going too well, or an editor stepped so far out of line as to affect the character of the magazine, intervention was direct and personal,

Pierre Brissaud 1931

Olga Thomas Wagstaff 1920

Irma Campbell 1922

retribution swift. The reputation of British *Vogue* in the early twenties as an intelligent magazine for intelligent people still stands today; but there was evidently a little too much of Bloomsbury about it and not enough fashion, and Dorothy Todd, the editor who was responsible, had to go.

As for the French edition, that set off at the sedate pace it has maintained for sixty years, except for the interval of the German Occupation, appearing once a month, secure in the knowledge that in Paris it holds the centre of the fashion world. In those early days even a steady loss was considered a price worth paying for its natural oracular authority and its ineffable chic; and yet it, too, remained deferential to the master in New York, supplying through its studio and offices the mass of *Vogue*'s essential matter, in knowledge, judgment, information and material.

Of the five American artists in Paris in 1923, Catharine Hopkins had been with *Vogue* for some years but was now a somewhat minor figure, and her Mabel-Lucie-Attwell-like drawings, mostly of children, were soon to disappear altogether. The other four were more notable: Porter Woodruff, the current specialist in *croquis* of the Paris collections; Polly Francis; Carl Erickson, who was to figure much more prominently within a year or two under the name of Eric; and the wife he had recently married, Lee Creelman Erickson, for the moment the more regular and prominent contributor of the two.

In London there were two artists: Frederick Chapman, whose time with *Vogue* was just about up, but who had set a distinctive example in his fashion illustration, unwhimsical, everyday, a style which others were to modify and develop; and George Plank, with *Vogue* for eleven years, and more to come, but whose fanciful graphic talent had long been reserved almost exclusively to the service of the covers, producing in his time some of the most extraordinary and memorable of them.

In New York were more of the steadies: Jean Oliver and Olga Thomas Wagstaff, who had served *Vogue* for a number of years in the most practical and necessary of duties, all but anonymously supplying the mass of stock illustration; Irma Campbell, another workhorse illustrator of long standing; E.B. Herrick, a general illustrator in the Chapman mould; Claire Avery, Robert Locher and John Barbour, all decorative and clever in their work and especially concerned with head and tail pieces to the regular feature articles on beauty and health, manners and mores, furniture and fittings; and Leslie Saalburg, of admirable versatility and unaffected observation.

In New York, too, was one of the most important of *Vogue*'s current artists. Helen Dryden had been a long-standing contributor, as prominent within the magazine as Chapman in London. But her career with *Vogue* was almost over, and her lively, consummately stylish and pretty aestheticism, an idiosyncratic confection of Beardsley, the Japanese print and Art Nouveau, all arabesque streamers, flat bright colour and cherry blossom, parasols and picture hats, was not to be replaced. Home-grown as she was, and among the first to set the visual tone of *Vogue*'s new look, she was evidently always aware of developments abroad and, rather more than that, quite prepared to demonstrate openly her sympathetic interest. No other of Nast's principal Americans was like her, and her work bears the closest comparison with that of the Frenchmen of the *Gazette*, particularly Paul Iribe and George Barbier. It is odd that she should have prospered while Nast remained so undecided about the others, and that she should effectively have bowed out while they for a moment held the stage.

Two of Dryden's New York followers, Harriet Meserole and Douglas Pollard, an Englishman, were like her clearly open to European example, and both were to make a substantial, even definitive, contribution to *Vogue*'s physical appearance in the coming decade as they went their separate ways, each developing a marked and powerful personal style as Helen Dryden's authority fell away.

Claire Avery 1920

Harriet Meserole maintained a constant presence throughout the twenties, as much on its cover as inside the magazine. Emerging from the decorative aftermath of Art Nouveau, by the middle twenties her graphic identity was clearly established, a delightfully mannered, disciplined simplicity very close in spirit to André Marty's calm and elegant sophistication, though she was at times prepared to lace it with something of Benito's harder, sharper, more daring line.

Douglas Pollard, almost more than any other artist regularly used by *Vogue* at that time, catches and fixes for us the essential image of a peculiar and distinctive age. His elegantly impassive ladies confidently outstare us, sinuously extended, thrown into high relief almost like figures on an ancient frieze by his inventive and exaggerated chiaroscuro and wonderfully simple and effective line. Again it is Marty's sophistication that comes to mind, and also much of Benito's gift for emphatic simplification.

E.B. Herrick 1920

Of the other American artists, Lee Erickson, Polly Francis, Porter Woodruff and, to a lesser extent, Leslie Saalburg are the unsung heroes of a transitional period. Woodruff and Francis particularly were the long-serving and consistent stalwarts, always professional and reliable. Both are, indeed, too easily overlooked; for behind Polly Francis's restrained, even at times severe, approach lies a graphic imagination never allowed its fullest scope. After 1930 she faded away over an extended period, the reliable creature of the back pages of the magazine, the dutiful supplier of pattern-book diagrams and *croquis*. It is a fate she shared with Woodruff, one which neither of them deserved. He was always less reserved in his approach, his line more fluently expressive; and though it would be too much to claim for him any positive influence, it is possible to see in his work, at an early date, a palpable hint of things to come.

Thus it was that Condé Nast's regular contributors did what was asked of them effectively and often memorably. By the end of the twenties his was a distinguished and influential international production, quite as stimulating in its visual aspect as ever it was through its literary and practical content. *Vogue* had grown up quickly; in 1923 it remained in many ways a pre-war magazine in design and editorial style, and yet three years or so later it was entirely of its time, freer, more flexible, and openly experimental.

Much of this was confirmed when Nast brought in Dr Agha as his art director in 1929, but it was Benito who had done much of the groundwork, persuading Nast directly by memorandum and proposal for new layout and typography, and by open example in his work, especially in the sequence of monumentally stark and striking Art Deco heads and figures that he drew for the cover over several years. He was still much in evidence, one way and another, and he had been joined in the middle twenties by another Spaniard, Guillermo Bolín, also the designer of some notable covers, who adopted a graphic process more fractured and dynamic than Benito's own but very close in style, spirit and Art Deco adventurousness.

Bolin was established in New York, and it was to New York that many of *Vogue*'s European artists drifted from the middle twenties onwards, some simply to explore for a while that strange new world, others to stay. Pierre Mourgue, a young associate of the *Gazette* group, was one who made the trip, and soon was being used with an increasing frequency, bringing to the American edition an unmistakable Parisian wit and flair.

Of the Gazetteers proper, Mourgue was the closest in feeling to Pierre Brissaud, sharing Brissaud's lively eye for a pretty girl, the swing of her hip, the swirl of her skirt, her turn of foot. Close, affectionate observation of life is the

Pierre Mourgue 1930

Lee Creelman Erickson 1925

Fish 1921

chief characteristic of the work of both of them. Both imparted a sense of great fun; but with Mourgue the spirit of the work is more forceful, the line less soft and suggestive, the colour more solid and emphatic. Mourgue, as much as any of Nast's artists, stands for the continuing vitality not merely of illustration in general, but of the French tradition in particular. He contrived to produce at every point in his career images that still read as among the most emphatically characteristic of their time. Mourgue was nothing if not up-to-date.

Towards the end of the twenties he was joined in New York by an even younger Frenchman, Jean Pagès, another artist straight out of the *Gazette* mould, and quite as lively. Pagès was to keep its tradition alive until the Second World War and beyond. He was even closer to Brissaud in touch and feeling, but brought to the work a speed of line, a cursive panache that was quite new and proved to be a decisive and lasting influence.

The later twenties and early thirties form a period impossible to summarize, and the pages of *Vogue* defy the easy and familiar tags and labels of the social historian, with his Roaring Twenties and Jazz Age, Crash and Depression. These were changing times and thus were all these things and none of them. In *Vogue*, artists came and went, obscure and shadowy figures, the visiting celebrity, the coming man, and were asked to work in so many ways. What conclusion may be drawn from the fact that so strong a tradition of satirical social observation was established, Ann Fish, the Englishwoman, being the early great exemplar, with her curiously conventionalized linear manikins, and Cecil Beaton, later on, with his more fanciful and quirky observations? And there was Mark Ogilvie-Grant, making the rounds of Oxford combination rooms, Soho clubs and Bloomsbury drawing-rooms, and Benito, Lepape, Charles Martin and Mario Simon regularly parading their considerable talents of hand and mind's eye for caricature. How well it all is done, how lively and entertaining it is; how much it is missed in today's magazines.

Again *Vogue* chose to surprise the reader with a sudden access of historical information, or rather to tease by withholding so much. In the summer of 1933, another identity parade appears; only this time it is not the simple, self-centred question of ten years before: 'What is it you like most, and about *Vogue* especially?' that is to elicit the individual responses, but something more inconsequential. 'Several times, we have caught our artists making furtive little sketches on the sides of the paper destined for a fashion drawing... wistful conceptions of what they would have liked to draw instead of what they were supposed to draw; women clothed in garments closer to the artist's thwarted ideal.'

The four pages devoted to this diverting article are not sufficient to feature the work of those current contributors with any generosity, or even adequacy. Rather it is in the light it throws upon that currency itself that its chief interest lies. Little clue is given as to where any of the contributors are: Porter Woodruff

Mark Ogilvie-Grant 1928

Libis 1928

is still labelled *Vogue*'s American in Paris (the only thing we are told about him); the newly prominent René Bouët-Willaumez is a young French Count from Brittany said to have been lately in New York – and that is all. Polly Francis, Pierre Mourgue, the Ericksons, Benito, Lepape and Woodruff survive from that first roll-call of 1923. Of those who have come aboard in the meantime, Bolín and Pagès we know to have been established for some time, Bolín indeed having only just missed that earlier listing. Beaton, too, was already something of a star, by now, though his contribution to *Vogue* would soon swing heavily over to photography. Libiszewski, signing himself Libis, had for several years been producing some of the liveliest incidental and feature illustrations ever to appear in *Vogue*. Zeilinger was used a little around this time, but remained comparatively insignificant; and there were the David twins, Marie-Rose and Marie-Blanche, whose *croquis* in the coming years regularly delivered the latest news of the Paris collections.

Roger de Laver erie had been a regular contributor since the later twenties, occupying a comfortable and even quite prominent position by the special nature of his work for *Vogue*. Until the Second World War he sustained that particular tradition of instructive or demonstrative illustrations, sequences of exercises, beauty routines, all manner of arcane feminine paraphernalia and processes. It came down to him in part from Fish, in part from Martin and Simon, helped along by Benito and Lepape: highly conventionalized, excessively linear and simplified, stick figures at their most sophisticated.

The gaps in that slight and amusing list of an article begin to claim attention. The simple differences between this list and that of ten years before are to be expected, for there would inevitably be many: Helen Dryden's association with *Vogue* ended in 1923, and Frederick Chapman, too, soon disappeared. In

Roger de Lavererie 1929

addition, there are all those artists who came, figured quite prominently, and went, in the years between: Lambarri, very much in the Benito mould, and Mury, another Benitonian; Fellows, Lemon, Patterson, all of the direct Saalburg and Lee Creelman American school; Joseph Platt, a master of the closely observed vignette; Bocher, an American, successively fashion editor and editor of French *Vogue*, who drew rather like Locher and in 1929 turned to fashion design itself and was soon well established as the couturier Mainbocher.

Of the artists of the old *Gazette*, apart from Benito, Lepape was kept on only for the covers he still produced, though they became fewer with every year; nothing had been seen of Mario Simon or Charles Martin for several years; and in 1933 a final cover apiece from Marty and from Brissaud were published. Other omissions are more surprising. Douglas Pollard and Harriet Meserole are notable absentees; in regularity, if not in quality, their respective contributions had lately been falling off. Given the impressive substance of their work for *Vogue* over so many years, such neglect is still remarkable; within another year or so, both of them had gone for good.

One other major figure is overlooked in American *Vogue*'s 1933 listing. Though copy and imagery were still in large part common stock, since 1923 the three editions too had been changing significantly, slowly perhaps, but acquiring and then asserting their distinct identities, as editors and art directors variously and gingerly tested their independence. Some artists thus found themselves virtually confined to the one edition or another. For British *Vogue*, from the late twenties onwards, its star illustrator as often as not was Francis Marshall.

He was an artist very much of the Brissaud and Pagès school, but distinctively English in the quality of his social observation, particularly in his trick of picking up the pointers of class and social standing that in England even today, let alone between the wars, leave so decisive a mark upon claims to elegance and chic. The French, more hedonistic, allow the display to speak for itself; but the English like to know just how things stand. To an Englishman such acuity is fascinating, and Marshall's descriptions of the British social round, the horses, the balls and the boxes at the opera, whether as marginalia to articles and features, or as the primary setting for his illustration of the mode, were among the principal delights of *Vogue* throughout the thirties. Born in 1901, Marshall had been educated for the Navy, but in the middle twenties resigned his commission, having decided upon an artist's career, and set out to study at the Slade School. In 1928 he was taken on by *Vogue*, where he remained until the war took him back into the Navy and off to Bath where he served as a Camouflage Officer for the duration. He continued to be active as a free-lance illustrator, though not, alas, for *Vogue*, until his death in 1980. In 1934, quite as versatile and accomplished as Eric or Willaumez, with reputation and position secure with British *Vogue* and an impressive body of published work to his credit, he was a major figure.

The two most prominent and important of the 1933 newcomers were René Bouët-Willaumez and Ruth Grafstrom, both of whom had an immediate and lasting effect upon the style and appearance of the magazine, not through any personal revolution or innovation, but simply by work so distinctly of its time. The two of them were characteristic, not of *Vogue* as it had been, but of what it was becoming. Their work was now more painterly than graphic, more direct and freely expressive in its statement than apparently deliberate and closely designed; it was redolent of close observation and immediate response.

Both had been with *Vogue* from the turn of the decade, and now stood alongside Mourgue and Pagès, Benito and Carl Erickson. The rest of that little band, of course, had seen the transition through at first hand, and had both

Francis Marshall 1929

monitored and directed its course, albeit more by instinct than by policy. By now all of them, even Benito, had come round to this subtle and delicate Expressionism, looking back in their drawings rather to the cursive and direct notation of Toulouse-Lautrec and Degas, and the rich simplicities of Van Dongen and Matisse, than to the tighter patterns of Art Nouveau, of Beardsley and Mucha, or to Cubist and Constructivist discipline and severity. They commanded the opportunities and facilities of *Vogue* at a happy moment, for at last colour had become available for editorial use, not just as an occasional indulgence, but regularly, to be counted on as a matter of course. American *Vogue* led the way, and by the middle of the thirties colour reproduction was the commonplace of a magazine enjoying a golden age.

Willaumez 1931

Georges Lepape sends Françoise off to the Opéra, as long, slim and statuesque as any Modigliani caryatid, the cynosure of envious if oblique attention in Chéruit's splendidly Oriental slip and low-draped frock. Editorial colour was rare in the early years after the First World War, and here, early in 1923, *Vogue*'s thirtieth birthday provided just the excuse for this and five other celebration plates set around a Prize Contest for the readers. Twelve of the latest Paris models had to be identified, their designers characterized and the particular fashion points described. The gowns themselves were the prizes. But though the fun is American, the mood is very French. The plates were shared among the artists whom Condé Nast acquired when he took over *La Gazette du Bon Ton*, the small and highly specialized magazine founded in 1911 by Lucien Vogel and his brother-in-law Michel de Brunhoff (who later became editor of the French edition of *Vogue*).

A Seat at the Paris Openings in the Spring of
1923. Patou began the pleasant custom of a
preview before the press. 'It was amusing to
note the enthusiasm of men whose business it
is to report battle, murder and sudden death, as
they hastened to send out cables on the rival
merits of organdie, crepe and taffeta.' Marty
takes us *chez* Dœuillet (left), the first of the great
Place Vendôme establishments to follow
Patou's innovation, where the fortunate enjoy
first these evening coats and daytime suits, and
then, of course, champagne. Benito takes us
into Prémet's fine and lofty rooms (right) for
this most sinuous of silk dinner gowns. And
what better indication of what to wear to the
Parisian 'Dancings' of early 1924 – Franglais is
nothing new – than Porter Woodruff's rapid
croquis (above): 'A Swinging Movement
Distinguishes the Dance Frock from the Formal
Evening Gown,' is *Vogue*'s current maxim, and
models from Lenief and Drecoll make the
point.

The Prize Contest of 1923 continues through its six plates and dozen models, following its young heroines through the mild adventures of their social day; and the artists, of course, enter into the spirit of the thing. Mario Simon (left) describes the pleasures and opportunities of the afternoon stroll; and Benito (right), somewhat more mischievously, takes tea, with due apologies, in the manner of his colleagues, Marty, Brissaud and Simon. Marty supplies the tea-party vignette (below right) to grace an article by Marcel Boulestin in praise of the British housewife, 'that noble and entirely unselfish figure' (1924). And Brissaud too appears (below), teasing the pretensions of the cultured classes, 'those artists and writers of talent who know how to dress, which is rare . . .', as he sees them gathered at the fashionable Salon of 1923.

'I would love to be with you, one very hot day, when one breathes and sighs like the swimmer who rules a hostile element': so, French *Vogue* reminds us, wrote Madame de Noailles; and the thought is as fresh as ever. Summers long ago were always so very hot, and behind André Marty's graphic sophistication (above and right, 1923) is just a hint of the Summer Frocks, *Vogue* thought, 'of our grandmothers': 'Once a year, certain dresses were taken from their chests, exhaling a strong odour of camphor, their trimming of flowers a little more faded with each inspection – like our memories of those who wore them.' Paul Poiret's costume in Bianchini foulard, over georgette crepe, is in the swing, Lucien Lelong's the white muslin frock behind the push, Alice Bernard's the piped, tiered and hammocked crepe skirt. Meanwhile, at the races (below, 1923), Pierre Brissaud's elegant young thing, dressed by Worth in handstitched white batiste, exploits her charm to keep seats for her friends.

Francis

Polly Francis, an American based in Paris, was never one of *Vogue*'s star illustrators; she was nevertheless most characteristic of her period. Her cool, serene figures, with their fine line and clear contour, so elegantly statuesque, are always recognizable. This, one of her very few colour plates, shows just how delicately effective she could be. It illustrates one of Doucet's great successes of 1924, the happy marriage of deep blue rep to Jouy linen.

Charles Martin was one of the gifted team of Frenchmen that Condé Nast acquired along with *La Gazette du Bon Ton.* Increasingly, his contribution to the magazine was more satirical than sartorial: and even here we may just detect a certain air of gentle mockery or tease. And, *chez* Lelong (1924), old rose and moss green are deliciously dissolved together in this ensemble. Vignettes by Porter Woodruff, Robert Locher and Guillermo Bolín.

Léon Bakst, temporarily forsaking the theatre for a simpler decoration, expresses his feeling for 'Primitive Russian Colour and Design' in a collection of new crepes, ten of them in all, hand blocked on heavy crepe de chine, and each one signed, repeatedly, at intervals of a yard (1924). Lord and Taylor made them up, and Harriet Meserole, the most instinctively Parisian and stylized of *Vogue*'s artists in New York, shows off the models. 'For ardent temperaments that long to express their vivacity without sacrifice of conventionality, these new prints afford an avenue of glorious escape in their brilliant hues and original designs, both of which are of unquestionable smartness.' A Storm of Approval indeed follows, and we can almost hear the thunderclap ourselves.

For long periods in the twenties, advertising alone sustained colour within the magazine; some of the most distinguished artists ever to grace the pages of *Vogue* did so under just such commercial persuasion. Jean Dupas (below, 1924), one of the greatest, if somewhat under-sung, figures of Art Deco, whose murals for the French ocean liner *Normandie* are now in the Metropolitan Museum in New York, worked for *Vogue* only at this remove; as did Kees van Dongen, sometime Fauve and one of the most successful of society painters (left, 1926), whose love of high fashion and the fashionable was as open as was his influence on such younger *Vogue* artists as Carl Erickson (Eric) and Eduardo Benito. The high-Deco drawing by Benito (far left, 1928) was commissioned by Stehli Silks; Dupas and Van Dongen by Cheney Brothers.

The shadows dance across the wall, and an invitation
to the party is sure to come. *La Mode* goes blithely
from extreme to extreme, and 'Five Feet of Fan'
almost conceal Benito's young lady (left, 1924); for a
moment it is the size of the fan that is its measure of
chic. Leafing through the pages of the magazine in
this period, there are moments when we might
almost be persuaded that life was itself a party, to be
conducted as far as possible in fancy dress. Mario
Simon's three young things (above, 1924) are at least
fan-less, off to their masked or veiled ball: a queen of
Egypt, a doctor from Molière, and a most dubious
cardinal incognito – Howard Carter, no, Lord
Carmarthen – perhaps not, but we are prepared to be
deceived. And the great cover-up continues with
coats and capes of wonderful generosity: Benito again
(right, 1924), with an ermine and velvet cape by
Callot to command the grandest of grand entrances,
in a stark woodcut-like image of almost Japanese
refinement; and Polly Francis (above right, 1924),
with a marten wrap by Vionnet of a more studied
amplitude, so cool and regular, it is almost classical.

The year 1926 finds a place for flowers and feathers in the autumn mode. Here Benito describes (left) an unusual ensemble costume of breitschwantz by J. Suzanne Talbot. But rather more than that, though it may be rather more cursorily suggested, *le tout ensemble* clearly extends to the interior arrangements of the entire room, everything so much of a piece, with clean, sharp lines and gentle curves, to set off the fashion. In 1927 comes Lee Creelman Erickson, steadiest of contributors (and for a period in the twenties, rather more prominent indeed than her husband, Eric), with Chéruit's petalled black velvet evening cape, worn for her here by the Marquise de Polignac (above). In the next year it is André Marty's turn, under commission from the French designer, Jane Régny, to celebrate tactfully the simplicities of modern design and functional living, along with the bobbed hair and short, fringed skirts of the Bright Young Things (right).

Of elegance and chic: this drawing by Porter Woodruff (below, 1926) illustrates 'The Subtle Quality That Expresses An Aristocracy Of Taste And Breeding'. There was certainly no beating about the elitist bush in 1926. Elegance, so American *Vogue* tells us, 'is the outer evidence of various qualities of mind and character and taste'; and, in its particular gloss to Woodruff's relaxed and languid image, it goes on to say: 'The chic Parisienne, like the chic woman the world over, finds, in her choice of clothes, one of the many ways to express her intelligence, her taste, her personality, and her background.'

A full year before, Benito's girl (above, 1925) is quite as bobbed and casual, but *Vogue*'s immediate concern is less with the theory of chic than with the latest fashion. 'In this striking frock, with its geometric design, one sees the newest turn that modernist art has taken – dress painting. This exotic thing was created by Chéruit for Madame Agnès. It is an evening gown of silver gauze, unusual with its long, close-fitting sleeves, and exquisite with its design in tones of lacquer-red, grey and black, painted by Dunand, one of the best known of the modern artists.' Back to Porter Woodruff (left, 1926): 'A Tight Little Hat Of Tulle Is An Evening Novelty For The Theatre, for wear in the motor to a party, for any of the evening occasions when a hat would be a convenience if it were not out of place.'

Georges Lepape, star designer of *Vogue* covers throughout the twenties, ever as delicate, witty and stylish as he was inventive, did surprisingly little illustration inside the magazine; and it is on the cover that we find his charming young map-reader, surely not lost, and very much *à la mode* – her daytime choice in 1926 'not the severely straight tailleur' but rather its alternative, 'the graceful ensemble' of frock and coat. For, as *Vogue* so rightly says: 'Every woman must make her choice and stick to it throughout. . . . Indecision in a costume is as weak as indecision in a character.' Ernst Dryden supplied a small amount of editorial illustration around the end of the decade, but most of his work was for advertisers, usually French, and for Jane Régny in particular: here are her summer sports clothes for 1928, '*pour le golf, le tennis et le yachting*'.

Not the greatest Age of Travel, perhaps, but the twenties really were the first age of general travel in reasonable comfort; and if the well-to-do made the best of it, then who would blame them? With Bernard Boutet de Monvel's incisive figures (left, 1925), creature comfort and the space in which to enjoy it make the yacht simply the most personal and civilized of conveyances. As for the clothes, 'With the successful assault of sports costumes upon the summer mode, Boivin, the men's haberdasher, has invaded the feminine realm and provides some of the smartest of the new sports clothes for the chic Parisienne.' Even the heaving, rolling, deep and dark-blue Ocean has a certain romantic charm, and Harriet Meserole's little mountain, far from putting off, could surely only encourage the prospective voyager (above 1926). For *Vogue* declared itself 'the world's most inveterate traveller. It precedes smart society over the beaten tracks to its seasonal haunts; it fares forth alone over untrammelled ways. Wherever your travel urge leads you, *Vogue* knows the country, climate, and requirements'. Meanwhile, on the tender at Cherbourg, in the autumn of 1925, Leslie Saalburg's two chic young things, so well wrapped up in their fur-trimmed coats from Lucien Lelong and Jean Patou, contemplate with equanimity the unknown joys of the ocean crossing, or perhaps the surer pleasures of terra firma.

Carl Erickson, who had recently adopted the signature 'Eric', now extended himself in colour (1929) with a cursive freedom that spoke openly of the example set him by such artists as Van Dongen and Matisse. With the exquisite plate by Jean Pagès, however (right, 1931), more delicate and discreet in its Parisian influences – Pascin, perhaps, rather than Matisse – we are already well set in the golden age of *Vogue* illustration, that time in the thirties when colour was first used with editorial generosity (though for the moment only in the American edition). Here Pagès, the rising star, lounges on the terrace after dinner in the company of two especially pretty girls, one in plain chiffon from Augustabernard, the other wonderfully blonde and smocked in pale tea-rose taffeta from the young Norman Hartnell.

For *Vogue* the sporting twenties were bound up with the study and admiration of the horse – that is to say, with the deeper study of the clothes in which to appear to be so engaged. Brissaud's pretty young thing (left, 1925), stepping out like a racehorse herself, is dressed for Longchamp by Callot, in a kasha cape-and-frock ensemble with many-coloured brocade to add to the gaiety of the effect, and indeed of the occasion. 'Each Different Type Of Sporting Event Has Its Own Type Of Costume,' so *Vogue* declares – and Fellows's trio on the grass (above, 1927) are indeed most sensibly and suitably set up in their tweeds, sweaters and jersey suits. As for Leslie Saalburg's spectator at the polo ground (above right, 1929), 'the modern woman maintains her own individual chic and is warm and comfortable as well' – the point being the matching rug that completes Molyneux's fur-lined tweed ensemble. In the park, Guillermo Bolín shows the spring's newest frocks, from Barbara Lee (right, 1926).

With access at last to full colour reproduction, and the editorial confidence to exploit it to the full – even carrying a picture across the entire spread – American *Vogue* in 1931 showed readers just what they had been missing all those years. Pagès, a young Frenchman in New York, rose to the occasion, firmly projecting fashion into the real world, his eye and hand always as fresh as

the spring flowers themselves. 'Somewhere, somehow, green should be in your wardrobe this Spring. You won't regret it. . . . Blue promises to colour the Spring landscape. . . . Everywhere, in and out of town, blue-and-white checks are the rage.' And the flower girl in her blue apron and yellow clogs turns her back to get on with the arrangement.

Douglas Pollard, one of the most consistent and stylish of the regular illustrators, drew for *Vogue* throughout the twenties and well into the thirties. Quite as much as any other single artist, he set the period tone of the magazine with his severely chiaroscuro picture of elegance, his models so sinuously severe and remote, set up as though along an ancient frieze. He was never bettered for clarity, and always his own graphic enjoyment and interest come through, never more so than when he is looking closely at the latest hats. Here is a sample of his work, as relaxed as it is sophisticated. In 1926 (above), 'the very authoritative air of city chic presented by this unusually important model from Reboux'; and later that year (above right), black crepe de chine and an asymmetrically flounced and pleated frock from Prémet – indeed, 'many of the smartest new models have sides that do not balance'. In 1933 (right), 'The Hat or its Decoration must convey an Upward Movement', as with Maria Guy's Parisian fez, and the two-toned feather toque from Agnès, with its feathers crossed on top. And in 1927 (far right), a straw hat distinctly novel in its deeply curved and drooping brim – from Marie Alphonsine.

Guillermo Bolín (right, 1931) looks back at the crisp graphic style of the later twenties, with its clean lines and flattened volumes; Eric (far right, 1932), looks discreetly forward to a softer, more informal and expressive manner. The clothes, too, catch the shifting mood: Bolín shows a woollen suit 'in a green that won't look subdued against rural backdrops', and a dress, jacket, silk scarf and country hat: 'Yellow and Brown never bore one in the country.' Bolín was a prominent and versatile contributor; his major part was in the innumerable incidental vignettes and illustrations that did so much to make *Vogue* of those days so characteristic of its time. From Eric a year later comes an image fully of the thirties: 'This is the hat that all the fuss is about, Descat's . . . ''The Amazon'', which you set on your head like a man's – only, unlike the regular fedora, this has that cocky roll and dip to the brim, that hard-boiled chic of the Australian soldier.'

The horse again, and the more active bucolic pleasures: 'Generally speaking, our gowns know no tyranny save that of elegance and the strain of giving expression to our rare and interesting personalities. There is, however, one moment when our clothes become a uniform. . . . The first thing to do is to choose your habit, and for this you are recommended to put yourself into the competent and sympathetic hands of, say, Busvine of Brook Street, or Goodbrook.' For hacking, 'you may give your fancy a somewhat freer rein. . . . Don't order jodhpurs unless you are certain your legs are your best point. . . . If the girl who really shoots is a good shot, she may wear what she likes and get away with it.' The four hunting vignettes are by Francis Marshall (1936); and Pagès (centre, 1932) shows us Americans more British than the British: 'Nervous horses – pink coats – rolling grasslands – anything but superb tweeds are rank outcasts in the mid-South country.'

Pierre Mourgue, another of *Vogue*'s young Parisians between the wars, was less fluid and spontaneous in his work, perhaps, than his principal colleagues, but always strong and forthright in design and image, his formal invention always graced by a robust pictorial wit. Here a characteristic pair of plates just as they appeared in the American 'Winter Travel and Holiday' edition for early 1934: the Tyrolean look for

skiing with chamois cardigan and wool plus-fours by Mainbocher, and, 'If you want to be utterly new, you and your young man dress alike in Knizé twin ski suits of native, flannel-like "Loden",' and jersey shirts. Or perhaps you would rather go South in knitted wools: 'You'd think the Olga Rosen tunic blouse at the right was cut out of material, so deftly is it knitted.'

'Paris Launches Mammoth Stoles', runs one headline (Eric, below, 1934); 'Lelong Piles Fur On The Sleeves . . .', goes another (Mourgue, right, 1933), ''Tailored Suit With Eton Collar'' says a third beneath a wonderfully stylized drawing (Mourgue, far right, 1934) of the most un-Etonian of neck linings imaginable. And if Eric's drawing is very much at one with the Eric we know, with its soft, fluent and expressive line, the two by Mourgue are as different as the clothes they illustrate: the one clearly possessed of all the dramatic and over-lit glamour of a contemporary Hollywood studio portrait by George Hurrell or Clarence Bull; the other, in extreme contrast, referring directly, in image and style, to the French popular woodcuts of the nineteenth century, the cheap and robustly patriotic *images d'Epinal*.

Ruth Grafstrom (left, 1933) acknowledges her debt to Matisse, but *Vogue*'s mind is on the capes: 'Practically any cape is good, but one that smothers your shoulders in pink ostrich plumage is superlative – and it doesn't cover up your nice spine.' Fashion by Molyneux and Bergdorf Goodman. From Jean Patou (Eric, above, 1933): 'Face to face, this little dress is pretty innocent – long sleeves, conservative neck, simple afternoon lines. But when the lady turns her back – a crepe dress unmistakably for dinner-party wear. It is called "Hermonione".'

René Bouët-Willaumez now appears, a young Breton Count already well established, if principally in the American pages of *Vogue*. His sharper line and more astringent colour make the perfect foil to Eric's equally free and generous, but softer impressionism. Most characteristically (left, 1933), he shows la Marquise de Paris, so expert in the art of self-centred chic, being dressed by Augustabernard in the newest sheath silhouette, a flare of sable weighing down the Bianchini velvet to increase the opulent drama of the gown. For, as British *Vogue* insists: 'Parisian women, in their attitudes towards dress, show the great value of egotism. Their far-flung fame in the world of fashion isn't due to greater beauty or even greater taste – it's their staunch "I am I" creed. They study themselves. They suit themselves.' And a year later (below, 1934): 'Slouching, slanting sharply down your nose, J. Suzanne Talbot's favourite toque, "Claude Monet".' Eric (right, 1934) draws Jeanne Lanvin at work in her Salon: 'I act on impulse and believe in instinct . . . I am carried away by feeling." Here she inspects her low-flared cape-dress of silver-barred black organdie.

Willaumez and Eric in 1934: RBW catches Schiaparelli's glamour (above), silver plumes frosting the satin surface of the snake-hipped lady below that dramatic Elizabethan ruff; the Empire furniture matches the mode. Eric is at the Blue Train Snack Bar (right) where the envious eyes of American *Vogue* discover fashionable London 'dining easily and quickly on the best cold cuts'. But British *Vogue* is more concerned with the tiaras: 'Granted – they are démodé, pre-war and all that; but then, on the other hand, England and Italy are really the only tiara countries left.'

Young Cecil Beaton, a mischievously acute observer of the *beau monde* between the wars, finds in 1933, in 'a country idyll . . . Mrs Reed Vreeland, noted as a hostess and a person of unusual charm, and . . . Mrs Sitwell, wife of the poet [Sacheverell]'. Far left, below (autumn 1929), 'Who would think this was June? Well, it is Lady Inverclyde, which is the same thing.' And how unfortunate it is that 'a bowl of lilies should obliterate the features of the Viscountess Curzon' (1928). His study of the Hon. Blanche Arundell and her spotted dog (1934) is more direct than usual, which helps to persuade us of its likeness.

1935-1946

*Romantic Expressionism and
applied Surrealism
Vogue's eye on society
in peace and war*

All periods are arbitrary, more or less, all of them in some degree transitional; and with Willaumez we now close one that in 1934 is quite as much in a state of change as when Lepape opened it for us those twelve years back. His lady shows clearly just how far we have all moved on, turning her back as it were upon the sharper, more rigorous geometries of the so recent past for the softer, longer, more delicate and gentle lines to come: her pink, coxcombed panama, so nicely tilted, from Rose Descat, the voluminous tweed cape ensemble from Augustabernard.

In 1935 the United States was poised between the Great Depression and the New Deal. Britain was apparently enjoying a long, late afternoon of Imperial sunshine, yet at home pulling herself slowly and unsurely out of economic slump and mass unemployment. The invasion of the Rhineland, Italy's African adventures, civil war in Spain, abdication in England, came all too soon. Through those few years of the late thirties, there was in the air everywhere a very real sense of old worlds coming to an end, younger ones, as unpredictable as ever and perhaps more dangerous, taking over. The energetic and uncomplicated hedonism of the Jazz Age had long before given way to something more febrile and more sophisticated, in art and fashion as in everything. The look was far less severe, the clothes and hair longer, softer, flowing more freely, the decoration prettier, the materials richer. The bracing, nihilistic stimulus of Dada had been replaced by the riper, more introverted decadence of high Surrealism – *pourriture noble* indeed.

The year 1935 found *Vogue* as committed as ever to the drawn image of the mode. If Condé Nast's doubts as to the efficacy of the drawn cover in selling the magazine were growing, they would appear to have concerned only the cover itself, for inside the magazine he presented a profusion of fashion drawings and paintings as colourful, daring and various as they were delightful. Benito, Beaton and Pagès were still conspicuous, as were Ruth Grafstrom, Marcel Vertès and Francis Marshall. Even Mourgue and Laveterie were not altogether out of it. Christian Bérard was the most spectacular and distinguished of the newcomers. In 1939 René Bouché appeared, destined to dominate two post-war decades. The later thirties were golden years. Their dominant presences were two rival, mutually complementary artists, René Bouët-Willaumez and Carl Erickson (Eric), now at the height of their inventive and interpretative powers.

Of the two, Eric could reasonably claim the seniority, for by 1935 he had already served nearly twenty years with *Vogue*. After art school in Chicago, he had moved on to New York in 1914, a young man in his early twenties, and for the next half dozen years he made a living of sorts as a free-lance commercial

Marcel Vertès 1935

illustrator, even selling the odd drawing to *Vogue*. In 1920 he married Lee Creelman, herself a fashion illustrator; she was for many years a far more significant contributor to *Vogue* than her husband, whose appearances long retained the distinctive character of what the bird books call the Irregular Vagrant or Occasional. The couple moved to Paris, which was to be their post until the Second World War; and though he appears to have been taken on to the staff in 1925, the major portion of his contribution was still advertising rather than editorial. It is not, indeed, until 1930 – by which time Willaumez had arrived and was increasingly in evidence – that Eric began to appear with any consistent prominence. By 1932 Eric and Willaumez were each as important as any artist on the books; and, whatever the nature of their personal rivalries, their careers marched together for the next twenty years and more.

But that long apprenticeship and comparative obscurity should not be too lightly written off. Quite how much the art student from Illinois knew of modern art is open to speculation. In the year before his own arrival in New York, the Armory Show had brought the work of the great masters of Impressionism, Post-Impressionism and the more recent avant-garde to a startled and sceptical American audience, but there is no indication that he was at all aware of the controversy. Even at the time of his marriage, when some idea of what was going on must surely have begun to filter through to him, if only through the pages of *Vogue* itself, what little we see of his own work shows it to be steadfastly graphic in the established American manner, unaffected and straightforwardly descriptive. If he had not cared to look again at those revolutionary Van Goghs, Cézannes, Matisses and Picassos, he was not the only American to remain aloof.

How very different it was within a year or two of his migration to Paris, when his work became manifestly experimental if for a while still tentative and uncertain. And by the time he began to win a more regular and prominent place for himself, it was unmistakably clear that he had been looking long and hard at what Paris, and the Paris School in particular, had to show him. He was

Eric 1930

evidently peculiarly taken with the graphic strain in the European tradition – romantic, painterly, cursive, freely stated, direct, apparently spontaneous – that so demonstrably links even the delicate intimacies of Watteau to the bold, frankly modern Expressionism of Van Dongen and Matisse. There was also the speed and astringency of Toulouse-Lautrec, and the calmer, more reflective study, though just as direct and deeply felt, that linked Holbein to Degas.

For a while it was the more current excitement that claimed Eric, especially in much of the work he did for indulgent advertising clients in the later twenties. The example of the Fauves and the Expressionists, a simple immediacy in statement and clean, uncomplicated, frankly decorative colour, was to stay with him; but his guiding sympathy lay elsewhere. In the work of his maturity, which was largely devoted to *Vogue*, the effect of Degas and Toulouse-Lautrec was plain enough. His, of course, was always a qualified, compromised tribute, but none the less sincere for that, and if he had sometimes to bend his talent to the vanity of his sitter, to the practicalities of the trade, or to the particular fancy or requirement of editor or art director, we should remember too, perhaps, that Toulouse-Lautrec submitted to similar constraints in working for the theatres and cabarets of Montmartre.

Eric, a late developer, was nearly forty in late 1930 when he designed his first cover for *Vogue*. It marked his emergence as a graphic force. From then on, he gained in confidence and sophistication, but his style remained essentially the same and unmistakably his own. It is all line, though it may be a line of colour laid on with a brush: a deft, subtle and suggestive calligraphy. The statement is simply made, pointed rather than exaggerated in its description of whatever happens to be the current disposition, the particular attitude, the elegant ideal. The image catches the passing moment with a gentle, sometimes even slightly mocking, but always friendly touch. The turn of the head, the cast of the eye, the flexion of the hip just so, all are registered by a softly modulated contour, now pressing more assertively, now passing lightly on. And if the clothes themselves are not always exhaustively examined and illuminated (which is precisely the respect in which Condé Nast held the Frenchmen to be inadequate), the whole effect is created nevertheless, conjuring up the thought of what might be possible, if only in an ideal world. Eric drew always from life, never from memory, imposing agonies of immobility upon his subjects. The lightness of his touch belies the efforts of study and application, and identifies him as a remarkable draughtsman in his special field.

With the Fall of France, Eric and his family escaped through Bordeaux and on to New York which was to be his base for the duration. In the course of the war he extended his range, reporting upon its circumstances and domestic history, drawing portraits of leaders, personalities and anonymous servicemen alike.

His undeclared rivalry with Willaumez continued for just so long as the younger man maintained his association with *Vogue*. In fact, they were lucky to

Eric 1935 >

Grafstrom 1937

have each other, for they were wonderfully complementary, each lighting up the other's virtues with his own. But Eric is unique in *Vogue* for what we are allowed to know of him, and for the implied affection in which he was held. Willaumez, in contrast, is a fugitive presence despite the central importance of his contribution to the magazine.

René Bouët-Willaumez, variously acknowledged to be a Frenchman from Brittany and a Count, first appeared in *Vogue* in 1929, a young man who had recently abandoned engineering for art and Paris. His early work was unremarkable, even pedestrian. Not having enjoyed the advantages of any formal training, he seemed to be making the most of a lucky break. His style in that first year or two was extremely close to that of the two Ericksons, especially to Lee Creelman's, still in many ways the more assertive and influential of the two. This, the sincerest form of flattery on Willaumez's part, was as sincerely resented by her. Consequently, as his star rose, Brunhoff, head of the Paris office, soon found it politic to send him to London and off the Ericksons' beat.

Artists are touchy creatures, understandably made edgy by any who dare tread too closely behind them; but the Ericksons had no real need to worry. Willaumez did indeed master his craft with commendable speed, but, of course, as he did so his own inalienable signature declared itself ever more clearly in the work. By the end of 1931 and the London trip, Willaumez's characteristic line, sharper and more incisive than that of any of his colleagues, and flowing with a more nervous energy, already marked him out. If he is close in style and spirit to anyone, it is not to either of the Ericksons but rather to Jean Pagès, who preceded him to New York, and through Pagès to Mourgue and Brissaud and the whole lively, elegant tradition of French graphic report and observation. It is perhaps reminiscent of Constantin Guys and Louis Forain; and, while Eric may openly acknowledge his great debt to France, it is Willaumez who will never let us forget that he is actually a Frenchman, *sportif*, *mondain*, ineffably *chic*.

Vogue, especially American *Vogue*, continued to use Willaumez extensively throughout the forties, but it was in the year or two just before the war that it made the most of him, and he rose to the opportunity. His gift was for a peculiarly dramatic presentation of the latest, the highest fashion, and for catching something, whether by the merest hint or the most outright and emphatic statement, of the inherent drama of *la mode* itself. His sharp and acid colour, so strikingly adventurous in its intensity and combination, deadly nightshade purple and green; his heavy tonality and often fierce lighting; and always his clean, swift, unhesitating line, thrown into a sharp relief by the cursory vigour of shading, filling, hatching: these all combined to set up some of the most memorable and evocative images of that distinctive period. The arrogance of fashionable elegance has hardly been better expressed.

Willaumez and Eric matured as artists together, sharing an aesthetic and indeed a practice; for their similarly Expressionist calligraphy served the same ends, their loaded brushes described the same fashionable world. But after that admittedly close beginning, and despite all those things they had in common, the sensibility was palpably not the same: the one ever fresh, a brisk and glamorous stimulant; the other milder, less demanding, more gently seductive.

They did not have *Vogue* entirely to themselves, however; and in 1935 they were joined by one of the great Bohemian characters of the Paris of the time, Christian Bérard. Still only in his early thirties, he was already the darling of salon, theatre and café alike, a central figure of the artistic *demi-monde*; and as such he was of course ever the stuff of contemporary memoir and anecdote. Of all *Vogue*'s artists he is the one most widely celebrated in the journals and incidental documentation of *Vogue* itself, its associates and habitués.

'Bébé' was indeed an extraordinary figure: fat, unpredictable, unpunctual, depressive, addicted to opium, but lively, witty, a manifest charmer; and, as is so often the case, the personality came very close to obscuring the talent and the achievement. It was not the particular qualities of his work that led Condé Nast to poach him from Randolph Hearst's *Harper's Bazaar* in the first place – for both Nast and Hearst made it quite clear that his work was lost on them, was far too advanced for the ordinary reader, and was impractical and undescriptive besides: it was his celebrity that fuelled their rivalry. As Nast's long-time principal associate, Edna Woolman Chase, remarks: 'It was politic to publish him.'

Willaumez 1937

That Bérard should have been as influential as he was is therefore the happiest of consequences. He was never a great painter, though examples of his work have filtered through into such major public collections as the Museums of Modern Art in both Paris and New York; but he was a remarkable designer: an artist, that is to say, who required the stimulus of a creative partnership with someone else whose words or music his own imagination might serve. His chief talent and great love were for the theatre, and over many years he sustained a most fruitful association with Jean Cocteau, whose *réalisateur* he was in ballet, film and play. For him a diversion into the world of couture was so natural as to be almost inevitable, and the highest fashion was always a kind of theatre. His strange, attenuated, perfunctory figures are forever on stage, set against the colonnades and arbours of his romantic vision: the mood, the suggestion, the effect, is everything. To ask for information would be to miss the point. He was indeed a romantic and an Expressionist, a creature of the latter-day reaction of the School of Paris against the stringencies of Constructivism and the Bauhaus, the wilful iconoclasm of Dada, and the excessive psychological indulgences of Surrealism.

Vogue's long flirtation with Surrealism had already begun by the time of Bérard's arrival, for it was very much in the air in those middle thirties; and in his work, too, can be caught something of its pervasive aura, a certain disembodied quality in the imagery, a sense of dislocation and arbitrary and

Bérard 1939

bizarre association as in a dream. But he never embraced the feverish precision, ambiguously literal, that so characterizes the work of the declared Surrealists. A generalized kinship was enough, and in the speed of his statement, in its spontaneity and his fatalistic acceptance of the mark that the moment required of him, he remained always the true Expressionist. His work, for all its prettiness and particular purpose, prefigures oddly much of the more abstract Expressionism, both European and American, that was to emerge so strongly in the forties.

Paris was Bérard's base, and, caught by the war, he disappeared from *Vogue* until the Liberation. The theatre, which sustained him throughout the Occupation, claimed ever more of his attention, and, though he continued after the war to produce work for *Vogue*, he was never again to be so persistent and significant a contributor. He died suddenly, early in 1949, aged only forty-seven, whether by his own hand is open to question, but most certainly physically eroded by the unforgiving combination of the fiercest energy, both social and creative, and narcotic dissipation. He was much loved and much mourned. His was the funeral of the year.

There were several other artists who made significant contributions to *Vogue* in this time before, during and after the war; and the most important of them, if not in terms of comparative talent at least in those of continuing and formative presence, was René Bouché. He, like Willaumez and Marshall, came late to the craft, and he was already in his middle thirties when he persuaded *Vogue* to allow him his chance. In 1939 his work was used editorially in both the French and British editions, and he also produced one of the prettiest covers of the year, the milliner's shop full of the summer's bows and flowers, ribbons and laces, straws and tulles. At the outbreak of war, so the story goes, he, a Czech émigré, joined the French army, fought through until the fall of France, suffered all the vicissitudes of battle, capture and escape, and early in 1941 reached New York at last. There he failed at first to impress American *Vogue* with his work, but had the nerve to ask for – and to get – a subsidy and six weeks' grace in which to practice.

Bouché's start had been late and interrupted, and certainly it was in New York in 1941 that his career effectively began. Immediately he made a considerable impression, which established him as a regular and expected contributor to the American edition. His work was then, and continued for some years, exclusively black and white, firmly and accurately drawn, and lively in the European manner of close observation and witty commentary and description. Frequently he was allowed to spread the single tableau of his design across the double page, and such emphasis and prominence would surely be enough to make some kind of mark; but with Bouché, to say so would be to belie the qualities of this early work, the vivacity of his line and his descriptive wit, which combine to make it remarkable.

The influences are natural and clear: Mourgue and even Brissaud at a certain distance, and of course, and most immediately, Jean Pagès, with the light characterization of his models and his cheerful sense of an occasion. Bouché was nothing if not up-to-date, and, in reference and imagery if not in style, he also paid close attention to the *tableaux vivants* of current and fashionable Surrealism, tricking out his compositions with gently forced perspectives, theatrically remote and generalized locations as on an empty and isolated stage, and with all the impedimenta, the dummies, models and lay-figures, of the studio and fashion house.

But this side of him was soon modified. By the war's end his mature style had declared itself, and he was confirmed in the romantic Expressionism, relaxed, disarmingly decorative and throwaway, that was to see him through. It is from this point that he stands with Eric and Willaumez in *Vogue*'s last great days of fashion illustration. His work would refine itself by degrees, superficially at least, but remain essentially unchanged. He would take chances perhaps, and even at times seem not to care overmuch, the drawing now more, now rather less scrupulous in its accuracy and graphic function, the paint perfunctory, casual, sometimes even thoughtlessly dashed off. Always there is the danger, in work done to meet a deadline, of too easy and seductive a prettiness of effect. All artists working to commission are vulnerable to such pressures and expedients; and Bouché was perhaps all the more exposed because of the comparative eminence and isolation that *Vogue* visited upon him in his last years. Like Eric before him, he was in demand, which was flattery enough; and his was the opportunity, even the obligation, to flatter all those whose dearest wish was to have their fleeting celebrity fixed by him.

It is much to Bouché's credit, therefore, that pushing his luck the while, and with no peer to test himself against directly in his last years, he should come back at us repeatedly with powerful and memorable images, especially when allowed the seductive luxury of a sequence of colour plates in which to indulge to the full his rapid, colourful and romantic calligraphy, his wrist loose and his brush loaded with watercolour.

Bouché died suddenly in 1963 and was regretted gracefully by *Vogue*. In the American edition there appeared an obituary notice written by William S. Lieberman, then Curator of Prints and Drawings at the Museum of Modern Art in New York; 'As an artist René Bouché chose a narrow field. Within it he developed superbly and became a master. . . . Eventually he became a master of social portraiture . . . the analysis sympathetic, but also quick, intuitive and penetrating.' And though the case may have been a little overstated, in the circumstances of the moment, it says as much for Bouché's spirit and ambition as for his achievement as an artist that the case could be made at all.

At that curious hinge or fulcrum of a period just before the war, Jean Pagès was one of the most important linking figures, not only between periods but in

Bouché 1946

Jean Pagès 1936

terms of cultural geography. Like Pierre Mourgue a little before him, he had been tempted across to the United States in the middle twenties, and he, too, had stayed. In his work he represents the Gallic strain of social commentary in the observation and description of the mode – delicate, affectionate, acute, always lively and accomplished – which Brissaud and Marty had refined before him, which Eric had yet to acquire at source, and of which Willaumez was to become the arch-exponent.

By early 1940 Pagès had all but bowed out for good. He returned in haste to fight for France, and through the Phony War he continued to do what he could for *Vogue*; his was the last memorable cover of the European editions in that early summer of 1940; his chic Parisienne, plumed and bonneted, walks through the Bois, the Allied officers briskly in step behind her. With the fall of France he disappeared from view until the Liberation. Thereafter, his reappearances were brief and intermittent, and all too soon he faded entirely from view.

Of all *Vogue*'s artists in any period, who were asked to address themselves regularly and substantially to the principal editorial illustration, Pagès' touch was perhaps the lightest: always charming, but never sentimental or coy, gently mocking but never allowing the tease to become sly, or indeed less than kind. His models are ever active as they swing along the street, or merely turn easily and elegantly, cocktail in hand, to talk to a friend. His work is overlaid with the mood of parties, gossip and light hearts. His hand is freer than his compatriots', his line as sure and confident as it is swiftly done. His work has none of the static graphic mannerism of Marty, Mourgue or even Brissaud, certainly nothing of the exaggeration of Benito or Lepape. More accomplished than the early Willaumez or Eric, as erudite a draughtsman as any of his colleagues, Pagès wore his learning lightly as he shepherded his bevy of bright young things through their parties and expeditions in those summer afternoons and evenings before the war, 'fleeting the time carelessly, as they did in the golden world'.

The war came suddenly, and changed everything, but not quite at once. The French monthly production schedule missed a beat or two, but *Vogue* continued to appear in France into the late spring of 1940, when Michel de Brunhoff at last took the hard decision to close it down in spite of German blandishments. Condé Nast at least had seen it coming, and already given his editor *carte blanche* to act as he saw fit: 'We are about to be cut off from each other. I know that you will have to make vital decisions. This is to tell you that I approve in advance every decision that you will make in the name of Condé Nast Publications.'

The United States was still a year and a half away from its own final commitment, and in New York the war seemed a long way away. American *Vogue* continued to appear regularly twice a month, and only gradually did the more serious aspects of the situation begin to impinge upon its editorial consciousness. There were incidental features and reports from time to time: the 1940 spring collections perhaps, and what was worn in the blackout in that

Phony Wartime. But Nast could not help worrying a little that even such detached observation of affairs abroad might disturb the American reader at home. It was not really until first-hand accounts, by his familiar contributors, of the Battle and the Fall of France, the flight from the Occupation, and the Blitz on England, began to come through that the editorial mood became by degrees more openly concerned, more serious. (It is only fair to say that American *Vogue* was if anything in advance of general opinion in this respect.)

It was British *Vogue* that seemed to register and adapt itself most quickly of the three to the newly threatening circumstances, calling perhaps upon the experience of a generation before. Publication was temporarily suspended in October 1939, and by November, already subject to the discipline of a severely rationed supply of paper, *Vogue* was cut back from the fortnightly to the monthly interval that was to be its pattern for the next twenty years.

How quickly the mood had changed from the high spirits of the summer, now a fading memory of a lost world! In May 1939 Lesley Blanch could indulge her 'Seasonable cross-talk' without a qualm: 'The Ritz is lunching a babel of tongues. . . . Little rickety gold chairs arrive in vans and are hurried into ballrooms. . . . There is a smell of petrol, expensive scents, strawberries and shampoo. . . .

Children evacuating Paris with dolls and dogs –
They each wear a ribbon dog collar with their names printed on it

Bérard 1939

Imagine how bewildering a cross-section of London chatter would sound to a listener-in . . . My dear . . . it's all done by yogi, my husband knows for a fact. . . . Cook says the whole secret is to sieve the caviare twice. . . . Isn't Tiny looking divine: I love his new hair-do. . . . After all, I said, who are the Czechs? . . . Maud says not another inch. . . . She says she won't be seen dead in her gas mask. I say she probably will be, anyhow. . . . Then I said to him, "Who knows best, you or Chamberlain?"'

Well, perhaps, just the shadow of a qualm.

Only a few short months later, Elizabeth Penrose, the editor, was spelling things out with an admirable firmness and clarity: 'Our policy is to maintain the standards of civilization. We believe that women's place is *Vogue*'s place. And women's first duty, as we understand it, is to preserve the arts of peace by practising them, so that in happier times they will not have fallen into disuse. British *Vogue* found this to be true in the dark years of 1914–18 . . . so, once more, we raise the "carry on" signal as proudly as a banner.'

The war was indeed British *Vogue*'s central, inescapable preoccupation, with an immediacy and insistency that the Americans at home could never really know. Mrs Chase herself remarks upon the extraordinary behaviour of the London staff during the Blitz, citing a letter she received at that time from the head of accounts: 'Several times a day the air-raid warning goes . . . the loss of time got so serious that now we take no notice of the warning: we don't run until we hear the guns, or aeroplanes or something of that sort.'

She goes on to say how it seemed to her 'that the British gift for understatement was never more striking, more poignant, and, to Americans, more incomprehensible'.

The effect of all this upon *Vogue* itself, now so very much an institution on two continents, was naturally profound. The processes of divergence between the editions, like continental drift, had been slow, even imperceptible at times, but had inexorably been going on over many years. Even so, with so much of the principal editorial matter held in common between them, under Condé Nast's proprietorial eye, there was certainly a positive community of spirit and intention. The war at a single stroke made that community impossible to preserve; and Nast's death in the late summer of 1942, with America's own war barely ten months old, removed, if not the possibility, certainly the driving will ever to restore it. Post-war *Vogue* would remain a family still, but never again so close.

Within the first year of the war Willaumez, Eric and Bouché were all based in New York. Though something of their work was sent back across the Atlantic whenever possible, it was always necessarily an irregular and unreliable transaction. Benito, Pagès, Bérard and André Delfau, who was becoming increasingly prominent in French *Vogue* just before the war, were now quite out of commission. This left British *Vogue* to shift for itself. There was certainly

Roger Descombes 1941

plenty to do, plenty to draw, and the old social comment and visual chatter were immediately translated into News from the Home Front, Life in the Services, How Life Must Go On. Here Cecil Beaton was in his element, though he was abroad more and more as an official photographer. Francis Marshall, who was now in the Navy, was finding that for him, too, this was really the only contribution, and ever more rare at that, that he could make to *Vogue*. But Feliks Topolski, a refugee Polish cavalry officer and a remarkable if idiosyncratic draughtsman-reporter, turned up to carry on this kind of work, carving out for himself a peculiar niche first in British then in American *Vogue* that he was to occupy for more than twenty years.

Francis Marshall 1942
'The Wren and the Vice-Admiral breakfast back to back at the Queen's Hotel, Southsea'

Fashion drawing was for the moment the most pressing problem, and *Vogue* cast about for a while, giving one or two unknowns a chance, notably the young Ruskin Spear. Then out of the blue there came another refugee from Occupied Europe to save the day. Roger Descombes appeared for the first time in British *Vogue* in October 1940, immediately became a fixture, and before long was producing the major part of the British material with his scratchily elegant and very Parisian image of the Mode. His style was a curious cross between those of Benito and Bérard, and yet rather more literally descriptive than either of them.

He left as abruptly as he had come, his work last being used in the British issue of June 1945. By then, French *Vogue* and its artists were back in commission; Descombes was no longer so prominent, and certainly not indispensable. Such are the chances of war; but his was nevertheless a particular contribution, peculiar to its time and place. For the authentic whiff of British *Vogue* in wartime, we might as well turn to his portfolio of drawings as to any other: utility suits, sensible shoes and rakish hats, a spirited foreign view of domestic, stylish resilience.

Bérard 1945

The years of 1945 and 1946 represented a necessary pause before the reconstruction, inevitably dwelling on the recent past. This shows as clearly in the world of fashion as in any other. *Vogue* stood in this curious limbo in the character of Michel de Brunhoff and his resurrected and restored French edition, which was not, however, to slip back into anything like a regular sequence until 1947. This, in January 1945, was *Vogue Libération*, a special number, Brunhoff hoped, 'worthy of our magazine of the past . . . the first demonstration of our recovered freedom'.

The cover is by Bérard, red, white and blue with a fine galleon sailing proudly across a sunlit sea. Inside, upon the luxuriously thick art paper, come immediately nearly forty pages of full-page advertisements taken by the great houses of the French fashion industry, and the tone is set: 'Our readers will find again the familiar names of great couturiers and manufacturers of Parisian luxury who have wished to take part.' Then there is a review of the part, or rather the many parts, played by women in the forces of the Allies; followed by the verb *Respirer* conjugated at length by Germaine Beaumont: 'I breathe, and

Bernard Blossac 1945

the air floods in over me, as if all the windows in the world were suddenly open, as if no more in the world was there a window closed, a door bolted, a barrier between the air and me . . .'.

And so to *La Mode*: 'The Importance of Frivolous Things', and an extraordinary clutch of drawings by Bernard Blossac, one for each year of the war, to show that the work of Couture and the chic life somehow went on, though the Nazi flag might be flying along the Rue de Rivoli, the Germans striding through the Place Vendôme, the soldiers waiting on the Métro platform. Such admissions were open to misunderstanding and misrepresentation, and the success with which French resilience and ingenuity fashioned so many silk purses out of whatever sows' ears came to hand upset some Allied opinion. To survive at all, let alone in style, can be a kind of victory.

Then, first with Blossac, and with Bérard and then Benito, there appear the latest Paris fashions, the silhouettes of 1945, the very latest hats, *les robes d'hôtesses*, unabashedly luxurious and indulgent for these freer occasions, the winter coats – which Benito shows off at the celebratory Picasso exhibition – and at last *Les Cahiers de Publicité Couture*, an advertising portfolio of drawings by Blossac, Delfau, and the newcomer René Gruau.

La Mode, so important indeed to Parisian *amour-propre* at this of all times, is demonstrated and celebrated, colourfully and clearly, in paintings and drawings. The camera is by no means neglected, but is reserved – perhaps instinctively in this special number, this editorial *chef-d'oeuvre* and collector's piece – for the purposes of broader cultural, creative and social affairs: a long poem by Paul Eluard with images of assorted statuary removed from harm's way to the parks of provincial France; the lights of the town, with Colette at her window in the Palais-Royal; the luminaries of Parisian art and theatre, André Malraux, Bérard himself in his studio; fond obituaries of the poet Max Jacob, who had died at Drancy awaiting deportation, and the sculptor Aristide Maillol; and at last an account of the clandestine press during the Occupation. Brunhoff, whose own son had been shot the previous summer fighting with the Resistance, could hardly be accused of trying to forget, to blur the issues, to draw the veil. *Vogue Libération*, a mere fashion magazine catering to a moneyed and exclusive class, stands as a remarkable and poignant document of its time and circumstances, without affectation or naïve indulgence.

Nothing that American or British *Vogue* could do could carry quite so much weight; nor did they try. With them, too, life had to go on: Brunhoff himself had tacitly acknowledged as much in publishing a serious piece by Eve Curie on the state of America and its attitudes as the war was ending; and another, more teasing perhaps but openly affectionate, by Jean Oberle, 'Les Anglais, nos amis'. And in his own editorial he said: 'As long ago as October '44, our sister publications devoted numbers of extra pages to France restored, wonderful pages put together by the old Paris group, now reunited, pages containing brilliant and moving articles . . .'.

Those other editions had begun to move on to other things, the American edition entering a newly positive international phase, reflecting unselfconsciously the late acceptance by the United States itself of the effective leadership of the Allies and the free world. American *Vogue* would still be very much the senior partner. And British *Vogue* had somehow to pick itself up, adjusting to the anticlimax of peacetime and the practical constraints of post-war austerity, the shortages and rationing that would never cramp its sister's style. The underlying seriousness of purpose, that had become part of its very nature in recent years, would persist, not heavily or pompously, but as a quality, a mood.

The artists responded to the circumstances of peace according to what temperament and opportunity allowed. If they could travel, so much the better; if they could return, better still. The curiosity felt in England for the Europe that had for so long been cut off was enormous, as indeed was that felt in the United States for England. There is more than a hint of the adventure that Paris represented in the importance and prestige that was visited upon the season's collections, and the alacrity with which the chance was seized to report them. Bouché was quickly back for the autumn collections of 1945, and as Willaumez was to do the following year, just as quick to send his drawings back by wire.

The return to normality also carried its own peculiar kinds of excitement, both private and very public indeed. The *Queen Elizabeth* made her maiden civilian

Benito 1945

voyage late in 1946, with Bouché aboard as *Vogue*'s special correspondent and relishing every moment of the trip – the fun and games, the pre-war style of living, the noise and spectacle of the departure from Southampton, and the even more spectacular arrival in New York. And there, in contrast, was Eric, sitting in Paris in that summer of 1946, telling *Vogue* that 'the only thought he holds close to his heart is to return for good to his beautiful house at Senlis, to tend his garden that was ravaged by the Germans, and to draw the new collections without having too often to rush back and forth between Paris and New York'.

The romantic, sinuous opulence of 1938, characteristic of those last few years of peace, is somewhat closer in spirit to post-war relaxations in manners and modes, than to the severer, more closely corseted geometries of ten years or so before. Here it is Patou calling the tune at the Paris Openings that autumn, so slim and décolleté, the chain slung low on the hips and draped with velvet. And it happens that this is the first we see of the work of Christian Bérard, whose association with *Vogue* all but coincides with the period covered by this second part of the book.

Benito 1945

Christian Bérard, a young Frenchman
making a name for himself as a painter
and designer for the stage, and indeed
already noticed several times by *Vogue*,
now appears (1935) by editorial invitation
for the first time. He immediately
established a significant presence, and
began an association with the magazine
that, but for the period of the
Occupation, continued unbroken until
his death in 1948. His is a romantic
expressionism charged with Surrealism,
direct even to the point of the perfunctory
in his statement, but always decorative,
always very much Bérard. Here (far left)
we see him not quite at his most cursory,
but certainly simple and direct enough in
his evocation of Vionnet's Shakespearian
mantle of heavy silk crepe: and his
confidence is matched by *Vogue*'s blithe
disregard for the conventional assumption
that the reader needs, requires, to know
the detail at every turn. But Bérard does
from time to time present a somewhat
fuller picture, even though it may be
more by emphasis than conscious
application: on the right a fine fluid
statement of Révillon's mink cape, and
the silver lamé turban by Reboux; and,
near left, a turban by Talbot, tumbling to
shoulder level.

The young Hungarian expatriate, Marcel Vertès, previously an occasional contributor, now begins to make more frequent, though always explosive, appearances. More recklessly, casually spontaneous than ever Bérard would dare to be, he gleefully fixes the foibles and vanities of the *beau monde* with a deliciously spiteful brush. Here (left, 1936) he captures 'that recurrent phenomenon, the perpetually adolescent mother and her daughter. Dress, make-up, coiffure so charmingly similar. They go everywhere together; are more like sisters, really!' And another of his women hisses to her companion (right, 1936): 'Straighten your necktie! Everybody's staring at you!'

'The New *Vogue*, please.'
'It's two shillings, ma'am.'
'I know, but it'll be worth it.'

Vogue declares itself with great charm through Francis Marshall's archetypal English lady (near left, 1936) and Alajálov's world-weary American newsvendor (far left, 1936). True to type, of course, the lady's home is her garden (Eric, above, 1936): 'To the woman who gardens this apron is a joy: it is made of striped jute – equipped with every convenience: a rubberized knee-pad, huge pockets, tabs for raffia, and clips to tether her shears and gloves.'

Eduardo Benito was one of *Vogue*'s principal artists in the years between the Wars. His most notable contribution, cumulatively a most considerable achievement, was made through the covers he designed. The drawings and plates that do appear inside the magazine, however, are always intriguing or amusing, frequently picking upon the graphic tricks and foibles of his colleague rivals, now Eric perhaps, now Willaumez, now (left, 1937) Bérard, with his stumpy line and vivid colour. 'Have a fling, occasionally, at something gay and mad,' urges *Vogue* – corduroy bloomer-suit, or halter-neck waistcoat of baby lamb, by Schiaparelli. And there is Cecil Beaton (right, 1937), as much at home down South as ever he is with the old Noblesse – Mr and Mrs Harrison Williams at home with their dogs in this Palm Beach conversation piece.

Willaumez (above, 1939), never afraid of the simple effect, with his delicately exaggerated ladies – just a sweep of the brush and an almost Japanese stroke around a shoulder and down an arm. For summer, 'White never fades, never streaks, almost never resents plain tubbing, almost always survives for a second summer'. And in Paris, that same last summer before the war, is René Bouché (right): Schiaparelli jacket and 'skirt draped like a pelmet', Marcel Rochas tailored dress and jacket, and Francevramant bustle.

These two plates of early 1939
show Willaumez at his most
devastatingly assured and
commanding. In them,
almost at the very last and
with so nonchalant a flourish,
he seems to catch the perfect
image of American high style
and self-conscious domestic
grandeur in those final years
before the war. Left: two of
'the entertaining new
nightshirt dinner-dresses'.
Right: with Hattie Carnegie's
housecoat of corded silk, 'The
new Directoire silhouette
influences even your leisure
hours. Rhinestones nip in
your waist; there's a hint of a
bustle.'

Accomplished drawing of this kind appears so regularly in these years that its easy vivacity and confidence of hand, and the fidelity of observation that it so casually embodies, are too readily, perhaps inevitably, assumed, and so overlooked. *Vogue* never was an art magazine, and the professionalism, the subtlety and craft of the artist must simply serve their turn and take their chances. The practical information is always there, though the artist may remain unseen, a mere functionary; and it comes across in all its detail as the page is turned. From Jean Pagès (left, 1936): Ivy Hudson's navy toque with its stiffened veil, and the tiny black straw hat beside it. From Eric, ever sociable, these 'pretty debutantes in their best dance dresses', raptly listening (above, 1940) to the young Larry Adler, 'lionized virtuoso of the harmonica, who plays for both symphonies and private parties'. From Francis Marshall, as happy at the theatre as in the hunting field, and always in the prettiest, the most elegant of company: the Charity Matinée (right, 1936), all black velvet and paradise plumes, opulent black fox and, behind, black gauze blouse and Scotch cap with clipped felt feather.

'Here is a lady's face just as Nature made it,'
or Ruth Grafstrom rather, as free and sure as
Eric but still quite herself (left); and, though
of 1936, it is nevertheless wistful, even
poignant enough to symbolize that fated
decade. But *Vogue* is more admonitory than
reflective: 'Don't grouse about your
defects. . . . Don't shut your eyes to
anything – try purple mascara; cream that
has real fruit in it; moustache wax on your
lashes; two-colour lipstick. . . . Don't go on
wearing your hair "that" way any longer.'
On, then, to Eric (right, 1936), whose young
lady is perhaps a shade more confident,
though hers is not altogether an
unquestioning gaze. She appears on the
cover of *Vogue*, as delicately charming as she
is simple and direct: 'Schiaparelli gives a
strong hurricane twist to her flaming red
velvet hat. The caracul scarf has dyed
streaks of bright blue-green through the
black fur (the dress-makers are becoming
surrealists). To climax all, wear the newly
chic kid gloves.'

War came, and in 1940 Paris fell; Eric and Lee Erickson joined the endless southward stream of refugees. 'Flight is too swift and easy a word,' she wrote, 'to describe so dreadful a thing as this. Exodus is better – slower, heavier, more painful.'

Two years later, with America in the war, Francis Marshall in British *Vogue* could relax the stiff upper lip (1942): 'It's cold and it's wet and it's blowing half a gale, but Second Officer Ponsonby doesn't care because she is going home on 10 days' leave.'

In the Paris of 1939, in the strange days of the Phony War, before the German offensive, Eric was recording how 'they shelter in the Ritz super-cellars in satin or wool pyjamas', and (right) how 'They travel bolt upright in crowded carriages, complete with rug and sandwiches, wrapped in Creed's plain mohair top-coat, hair held in Agnès' night-cap jersey turban.'

130

Late in 1941, Willaumez and Eric together in American *Vogue*, the one as arrogantly as the other is relaxedly stylish; and bravura performances from them both. Throughout their time with *Vogue*, and especially in the earlier years, they stimulated in each other the keenest rivalry. Left, Willaumez: a coat for autumn. Right, Eric: 'if you ever feel inclined to belittle the importance of your shoes to your *tout ensemble*, watch a man's eye appraising a woman.'

There is a war on, but London life somehow continues, perhaps even more sociable and high-spirited than ever. In the pub, at the Hippodrome, at the Café de Paris and the Embassy Club, Feliks Topolski finds 'Behind the black-out – lights, dazzling by contrast, heightening the laughter, the music and the gaiety. Every place packed with youngsters and uniforms, lightly treading the tight-rope of the present' (this page, early 1940). Cecil Beaton (right, 1941) shows 'The way things are at the Dorchester – Roof spotters stand sentinel above', and as for the guests, 'some dress – some don't; some wear hats – some don't', and they all dance to Lew Stone's band.

DON'T HELP THE ENEMY!

Eric in 1944 (left), if anything even more prettily and fluently romantic than usual. 'When summer turns on its million-watt sun in America, you always want a hat between you and its scorching rays. . . . This summer . . . its brim will have less wing-spread than yesterday's cartwheel, its trimming will be more contrived, more deliberately pretty, its colour borrowed direct from a flower catalogue, its dimensions prescribed by Millinery Regulations . . . Reine's pale blue rough straw hat planted with roses, veiled closely.' But in 1941 there was nothing of restriction and regulation, and little of summer, about the ostrich fronds on Lilly Daché's vivid felt portrait hat, her natural stone marten stole, or her 'Poppy' lipstick – Willaumez, too, on top of his form (right).

R.J. Descombes turned up from Paris early in the war, and signed on for British *Vogue* for the duration, only to disappear as suddenly at its end. His decoratively scratchy, attenuated figures remain very much of the period, as evocative as any of *Vogue* in wartime – and the military are everywhere, the essential prop and supporting cast (left, 1943). For Bouché too, by 1945 very much the regular (right), they are irresistible, here shopping for a watch in Dunhill's with Claire McCardell's spindle-waisted tweed – an odd, informal foretaste of the New Look. But what a sad little piece of reportage by him from an immediate post-war Paris (left, below), full of bewildered, alien servicemen walking the streets for hours on end, victims of infinite and impenetrable mutual misunderstandings: 'Every Frenchman who has seen a "zig-zag" American soldier . . . considers himself an authority on Americans . . . Living on his own soil, with his own family, he has no clue to the loneliness and lostness behind that tipsy "zig-zag". The soldier, unknown and unknowing, has no key to the Frenchman's instinctive reservations about strangers, nor to the basic importance to the French of thrift, conversation and food. The soldier would like to share the last two, but the doors of restaurants and of language are both closed to him.'

Two pages of Eric, as grand and versatile as ever. They appeared in American *Vogue* late in 1943; Christmas was coming on and there was no knowing what 1944 would bring. No doubt everyone needed cheering up: 'Give her pearls . . . not just an anonymous little strand that she might fasten on automatically,' but great big ones, 'like these' (left) – and the image was memorable enough to be revived as a cover to British *Vogue* early in 1946. And there is the blouse in silk and satin, almost a tunic with its moulded shoulders and slender waist (right). 'The suggestion of a bustle in its double puff, its elegance and hauteur and sauciness are very Boldini. . . . Wear it with a perfume with a high esprit, such as ''Escape'', a satin perfume heady as more champagne in the ice-bucket and a whirl on a polished floor.'

Bouché more restrained and more informal than he usually appears. These pages from his notebooks present his material as it is taken down, directly observed, objective, the graphic ideas still turning over in the artist's mind. Here (above, 1944) young casual clothes for the country – waistcoats, shirts, plaid skirts, high socks: and Mrs Douglas Fairbanks (right, 1943), once Lady Ashley, acting the clothes-horse in Molyneux glen-plaid suit and jacket dress.

And now the war is over. Michel de Brunhoff, the editor, closed down the French edition of *Vogue* in the summer of 1940 and maintained his silence until the Liberation. Not all of his artists could get away; and many of those who remained kept up their observation of the mode, the German indifferently replacing the Allied officer in the supporting cast on the Paris street. But that is all behind them in this first winter of the peace proper; and yet how curious it is, in this splendidly overcast double plate, that Pagès not only should describe so forcefully *La Ligne Droite*, the Piguet coat and Molyneux suit and dress, all still so redolent of the military tailor, but also hark back to the spring of 1940 (above) and his last *Vogue* cover before the Fall of France, and to the towering feather in a Rose Descat pill-box hat.

America was always physically far enough removed from the War for life at home to go on more or less as it always had; and going off to Florida for winter sunshine was always part of it. On the surface there is little to choose between the holiday moods that Dagmar, Willaumez and Bouché catch, for all that they are set worlds apart: In wartime (Willaumez, below, winter 1943; Bouché, right, summer 1942), even *Vogue* was constrained by circumstances – 'The Government scowls at frivolous migration' – and had to explain that, even if the winter resorts were crowded, the reasons were honourable. 'Some women have closed their fuel-devouring houses in the North, have taken their children . . . where sun is the fuel. . . . Many more have gone to be near their husbands.' The war once over, *Vogue* was quite its old self again (Dagmar, left, late 1945): 'The famous jersey jumper . . . with a skirt it can fly south under a mink coat; can lunch under nothing but the sun. . . . Add a skirt and wear it to cocktails.' Here for the first time we come upon Dagmar's flat, dramatic style.

Eric and Bouché together now; theirs was to prove the principal, if again undeclared, double act of the immediate post-war decade in *Vogue*, just as Eric's with Willaumez had been for a dozen years past. And this somewhat acid green would seem to be a shared preoccupation for the two of them in 1945, with Eric's spring green lady (left) in the very complementary pink of perfection – hat and dress by Tatiana du Plessix. And Bouché is in Paris in the autumn to show us costumes that highlight the evening news of the collections: 'Lelong's slender black velvet tube, moulding every curve of the figure and crowned by a tea-rose satin Romney portrait drapery'; and 'a dinner suit by Balmain.'

Post-war Paris, and in gently
ironic contrast, a glance back
to wartime New York:
Delfau's daytime Parisienne
of 1946 (far left), just a little
sad perhaps, and certainly
'fully preoccupied with the
seriousness of life' – and
Willaumez's immaculate
New Yorkers of 1944 (near
left and right), as determined
as they are elegant.

The Royal Mail Ship *Queen Elizabeth*, the greatest liner of them all, was launched before the war but just a shade too late to grace that golden age of ocean travel. She made her maiden voyage as a troop ship, and continued to serve as such through sixty crossings. When at last, late in 1946, she came to make her peacetime debut in her true role, it was naturally something of an event. René Bouché was only one of some sixty correspondents who were working their passage. It turned out to be, he says, 'a refresher course in luxury, leisure, and how to enjoy them. . . . Confronted by so much . . . it was hard to relax completely. . . . After eleven, when the dancing started, there remained a surprised primness. In the evening the women consciously dressed down, most of them in long black sheaths with few jewels in evidence (they looked more dashing in the day in their magnificently cut tweeds). There was nothing to do, and that was enough to keep everyone doubly busy. . . . Whether to have a facial or a shampoo or was there time for both. Whether to play deck tennis, or squash . . . or bridge. . . . Which of the six bars to meet in. . . .' All Southampton had seen her off, and all New York turned out to greet her as she tied up at the flag-festooned pier. 'It was a celebration, an international première', a fresh start.

Traffic across the Atlantic was not all one way; and Willaumez was in Paris for the autumn collections of 1946, sending back by wire his drawings of Schiaparelli's latest look, and vignettes of Paris to set the scene and mood. The wire technique, newfangled and not altogether unsympathetic, has a certain simplifying and generalizing effect, however, and it is curious to see his line, usually so swift and incisive, softened somewhat (this page) almost to the condition of Bouché's. Bouché himself (right, 1945) had been there before him anyway, by a full year – and with news of Schiaparelli under Directoire influence.

SCHIAPARELLI

DIRECTOIRE

SCHIAPARELLI

PERUGIA

SCHIAPARELLI
SILHOUETTE

155

Eric in two moods in 1946: in spring as simple and direct as he will ever be (left and far left); and then (right) a grand dress for midsummer, and as grand a drawing, a full-blown Eric at his most gently characteristic. Indeed, *Vogue* was even moved to say so: 'Eric makes fashion move . . . makes the women move within the clothes he draws. Elegant women, who even lounge in the grand manner.' And those clothes: in America, bulky, colourful, well-cut evening coats, a specifically American fashion of the moment; in Paris, hobble skirt and dolman wrap from Lucien Lelong.

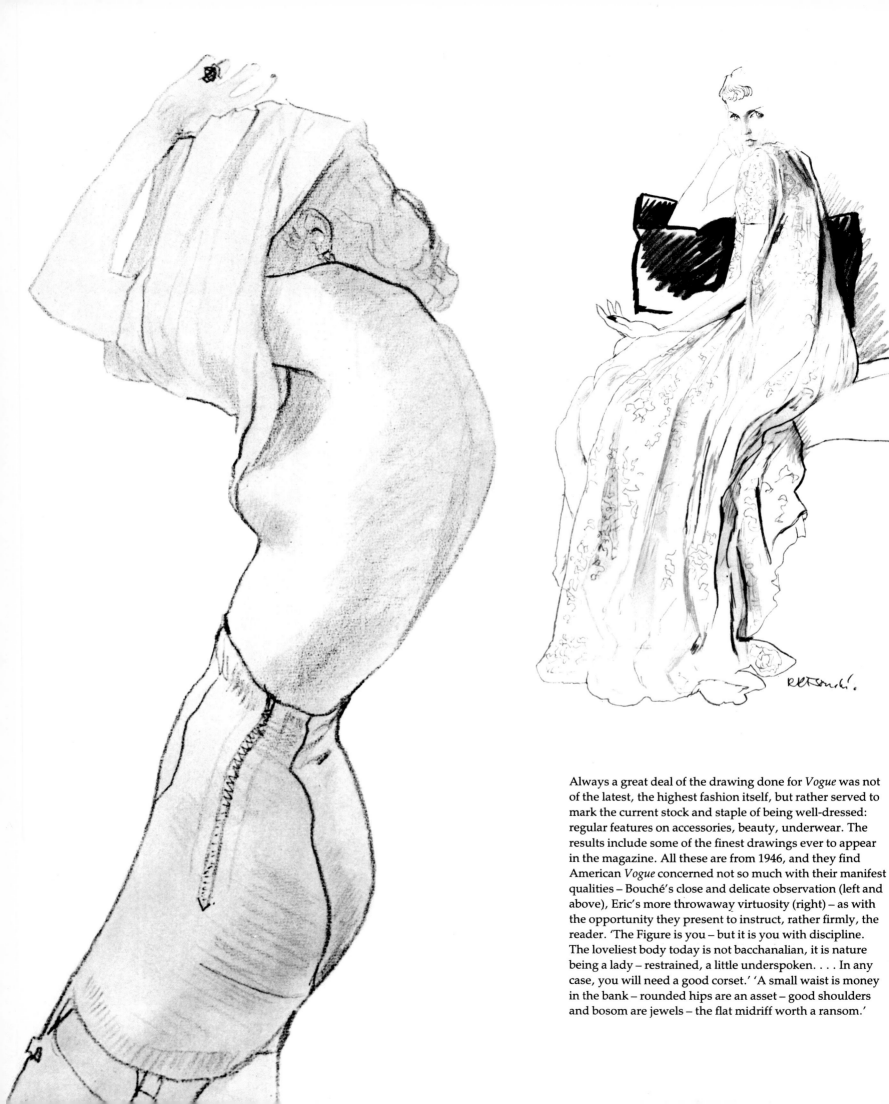

Always a great deal of the drawing done for *Vogue* was not of the latest, the highest fashion itself, but rather served to mark the current stock and staple of being well-dressed: regular features on accessories, beauty, underwear. The results include some of the finest drawings ever to appear in the magazine. All these are from 1946, and they find American *Vogue* concerned not so much with their manifest qualities – Bouché's close and delicate observation (left and above), Eric's more throwaway virtuosity (right) – as with the opportunity they present to instruct, rather firmly, the reader. 'The Figure is you – but it is you with discipline. The loveliest body today is not bacchanalian, it is nature being a lady – restrained, a little underspoken. . . . In any case, you will need a good corset.' 'A small waist is money in the bank – rounded hips are an asset – good shoulders and bosom are jewels – the flat midriff worth a ransom.'

1947-1983

*A New Look and a continuing
graphic tradition
From constant practice to
occasional use*

And finally, in December 1946, at the
very end of this period that spans the
war, Christmas in Paris for American
Vogue: a 'ballroom scene introducing to
America the charmed work of Lilla de
Nobili, young Italian artist', who offered
in particular her impressions of the latest
work of Mad Carpentier, Schiaparelli and
Paquin. She continued in this romantic
and theatrical vein for a year or two yet,
mostly in the pages of French *Vogue*; and
if her painting is immediately rather
Bérardian in its flavour, it also surely
looks back consciously to high
Impressionism, to Degas's dancers in the
wings, and the débutantes and ingénues
of Renoir. The theatre soon claimed Miss
de Nobili, and her distinguished career as
a designer for the stage, in Paris
especially, has continued to this day.

De Nobili 1947

Bérard 1947

Spring 1947, and with it came the New Look, Christian Dior's apparent revolution, a fresh start for the Western World and most especially for lately embattled Europe. Is it indeed the New Look that marks the epoch, bringing in with such an elegant swing the extended period known familiarly as 'since the war'? It was a very pretty look, but its extravagance seems now to be mild enough – habituated as we are to every novelty, from frank immodesty to the wildest, most inconsequential heaping up of material. Certainly, waists had been pinched in before, and skirts puffed out upon layers of petticoat. But the New Look made for memorable images, and *Vogue*'s artists were to continue as happily as ever in their accustomed interpretative and descriptive role.

In New York, early in the war, Alexander Liberman had taken over from Dr Agha as art director, and there were new photographers only too eager to make their mark under his dispensation; but surely there would always be room in *Vogue* for painting and drawing the fashion and the fashionable. Eric, Willaumez and Bouché were the established, but not quite the dominant, triumvirate. The war had confirmed the distinct and separate identities of the three editions, and *Vogue* entered a period which was to see no editorial or managerial initiative to bring them closer together. Few artists, or indeed photographers, would embrace them all with any consistency, and when they did it was only for an occasional, brief spell. For each of the editions, British, American and French, there was a markedly different, in most respects an exclusive, supporting cast, with those principals themselves by no means irreplaceable, and Willaumez in particular hardly ever straying on to the European pages.

In the late forties, French *Vogue*, much more than any of the others, sustained and celebrated illustration, as much for its own sake as for its useful description of the mode. The covers of French *Vogue* in this time were peculiarly expressive of this distinctive attitude, invariably drawn or painted, and, unusually for *Vogue*, reserved entirely to the one edition. Its artists were inclined to be similarly exclusive, and as prolific of editorial illustration as Michel de Brunhoff allowed or required them, at least for the remainder of the decade. Back into a regular schedule with the New Year of 1947 and six issues for the year, shifting up to ten issues thereafter, French *Vogue* even now retains something of the special flavour, at once definitive and celebratory, that characterized the first four issues of its restoration.

Although for a while drawing preserved if anything an even stronger presence within the magazine's pages, the artists' names were much changed, and then markedly inconsistent. Of the great pre-war names, Benito flickered briefly but did not survive that initial post-war flurry, and Jean Pagès too made only one subsequent appearance. André Delfau also faded quickly, and so did Bernard Blossac, who seemed for a moment about to establish himself as a major figure. Odd names from the past cropped up occasionally: the errant Descombes at midsummer 1947; Roger de Lavererie at Christmas 1948. Marie-Rose David had quietly made a fixture of herself, the steady supplier of the *croquis* of the collections until well into the fifties.

Christian Bérard was the most conspicuous loss to the magazine, and perhaps the most surprising, after all the efforts to secure him before the war. But his heart was evidently torn between painting itself, pure and private, and the more public preoccupations of designing for the theatre and the cinema. His collaboration in particular with Jean Cocteau produced masterpieces, and *La Belle et la Bête* is a kind of monument. Something of his work did appear in the magazine regularly at first, but the last single spread at Christmas 1948, a bare two issues before his obituary, was also the first he had supplied for sixteen months.

Vogue's own peculiar taste for a romantic Expressionism (called neo-romanticism), liberally laced with Surrealism, was never Bérard's alone to satisfy, however. Just as in the past such artists as Benito and Vertès had glossed and commented upon what he did, and had made their own distinctive contribution besides, so now others were seen to serve just as well, if a little differently. *Vogue*'s indulgence certainly survived Bérard's going. The exercise naturally took different forms with each of the national editions, but of the three the French was perhaps the most notably whole-hearted, various and adventurous.

Coltellacci, with his decorative bizarreries, the headless mannequins, silked and crinolined, at some strange *fête champêtre* at the world's end, and Denise Nicollet, more modest but quite as elegant in her attenuated, spidery romanticism, are both as characteristic as any of *Vogue*'s artists of this transitional yet entirely distinctive period. But it is the young Lilla de Nobili who is the most notable, and in spirit and feeling the closest to Bérard. For too brief a moment she appeared to be his natural successor, her work as freely suggestive as his if perhaps a degree more realized and particular, and more lushly romantic. But the Parisian theatre claimed her, too, and far too quickly. Her work for *Vogue*

Marie-Rose David 1950

Tom Keogh 1947

hangs in the memory far more persistently than its actual incidence might warrant, earnest indeed of its quality and her manifest ability to take her chance. Her career in the theatre has continued to the present.

It was another newcomer who effectively filled the gap that Bérard left. An American, Tom Keogh, burst on to the cover of French *Vogue*'s Christmas issue for 1947, and for the next four years he maintained a conspicuous and continuous presence in its pages, before disappearing as abruptly as he had arrived. It is remarkable that only the French were allowed to enjoy his fluent, often extravagantly pretty images. From Bérard, Keogh may well have picked up the confident, throwaway simplicity of statement, the disembodied decoration that was said to be Bébé's feverish drops of sweat conjured on the page into birds, petals, arabesques. There is also the free projection, the figures cast out into an elegant, seductive limbo. But there is nothing of Bérard in Keogh's wonderful graphic panache, all wrist as it were, and the lightest flick of the brush to close off the flow of the loaded brush. He is at times as crisp as Willaumez, as disarmingly sophisticated as Eric, as clean and swift in his line as ever Pagès, or Bouché or René Gruau, could possibly be. In addition, there is that most modern feeling and sensibility, caught perhaps from the extraordinary *papiers collés* of Matisse's old age, the colour laid on pure and uninflected, as flat, sharp and clean as though it had been trimmed with scissors. In this he was closest to Dagmar of American *Vogue*, and between them they established a manner that would remain conspicuous until *Vogue*'s editorial abandonment of illustration in the early sixties.

Keogh brought together what for so long had been various and divergent: the elegant applied Impressionism of Willaumez and Eric on the one hand, set against the relaxed graphic Expressionism of Bérard, overtly romantic and tacitly surreal, on the other. From then on, the middle ground was to be fully occupied; and in the work of Gruau and then Hervé Dubly in France, Vevean, Larson and Marcil in America, and Draz, Bouret and Eric Stemp in England, the strategic advantages of the position were clearly demonstrated, virtues so readily available on all sides – the perfunctorily stated, fractured figure, the swash of colour, the swift, light expressive line.

For all that, however, a committed idiosyncrasy will always tend to confer the greater, more positive distinction, should it ever be given the opportunity and encouragement to develop. The caveat hangs upon editorial courage, and it is with Tom Keogh in the four years or so around the turn of the forties and fifties that the last of *Vogue*'s graphic innovators appears on the scene.

The others all flatter for a while, not to deceive, nor even to disappoint, but simply to do the job with consistent professionalism and then move on. They are among the last to enjoy anything like a regular commission, but none is elevated to replace each star as he fades away or dies, none is given the chance to earn an international reputation in the old way, whatever his abilities or potential.

Eric 1954
An interview with Chanel

With Keogh gone, René Gruau is perhaps the most promising and sure to rise. He had emerged at the end of the war, his work clearly influenced by Willaumez, and quite as crisp, confident and incisive; but within only a year or two he was confirmed in his mature style, heavily chiaroscuro, the flat black areas of tone often modulated by the ink spattered on, as it were, by the flick of a toothbrush in the manner of the lithographs and posters of Toulouse-Lautrec, the silhouette and contour emphatically simplified, the line easily and elegantly turned. His were the very icons of post-war elegance: but already he was as much committed to the prestige advertisement of Parisian couture, particularly to the products of the new House of Dior, as he would ever be to any magazine, and such connections had always made *Vogue* uncomfortable. Gruau's work for *Vogue* remained occasional, as it does to this day, and almost entirely reserved to the French edition.

British *Vogue*, in the decade and a half before 1960, promoted no single artist to such prominence. More than the other editions, it monitored the real though infinitely subtle and deceptive decline in the editorial use of fashion illustration and its consequent atrophy as an effective graphic discipline. In those first years of post-war austerity, of the three editions the British had seemed to suffer most, apparently taking the longest to recover, and never in fact regaining the

John Ward 1949
'The Royal Academy's Annual Soirée'

amplitude of those far-off thirties. The luxury of twenty-six issues in the year, so long taken for granted and only given up for the stricter twenty-four at the New Year of 1939, was now gone for good, and for a while the magazine's monthly appearance was to remain the most straitened of the three. It preserved jealously, however, its own particular distinction, and for ten years or more no magazine could have possibly been more deliberately, gleefully, innately British, with featured writing to match the photographic ebullience of Norman Parkinson, and the quieter but nonetheless exquisitely characteristic graphic descriptions of John Ward.

Fresh from the Royal College of Art, Ward was picked up by *Vogue* in the late forties and celebrated, if only locally, as no British draughtsman had been celebrated before, occupying just the same interval and enjoying quite as much exposure as Keogh across the Channel. But Ward's heart was never in fashion illustration, though it served as a useful and seductive temporary expedient. His ambition was to be an artist, *tout court*, and indeed he has proved successful in his subsequent career, in the academic English way: Royal Academician, portrait painter to the County and topographical observer of decided gifts. He is no great original; but at his best, which is at his most informal and direct, he displays a technical command, finesse and sympathetic descriptive economy that few among his contemporaries can match. It is ironic that British *Vogue* should have caught him so young, and elicited from him, unselfconscious and off his guard perhaps, some of his best, liveliest and most characteristic work. Early on, there is much of the neo-romantic about him, but deeply marked by a scrupulous technical probity, a decorative richness, not unlike that of Lilla de Nobili, but rigorously set up and secured by the closest observation, and the most exact description. It is a romanticism closer to Watteau and the eighteenth century than to the indulgences of any later generation.

Ward is as close and accurate in his suggestive evocation of the English scene, into which he projects his descriptions of the passing peculiarities of the mode, as ever he is in establishing for us the fact, the detail, of whatever it is he confronts. He arrogates to himself, as all true artists do, the times he lives in, and records something which we experience in our memory only through his eye. Henley, Lord's Cricket Ground, the Fourth of June at Eton; or it may be Simpson's in the Strand, or the Savoy Grill, or again a family Christmas party in the country – whichever it is, Ward's fine, delicate, teasing line still conjures up for us by its peculiar flavour and suggestion a most lively and particular picture of British life as some were lucky enough to live it in those last years of King George VI: strawberries and cream on the river bank, and roast chestnuts in the fire.

Ward supplied as precise and informative a description of what could or should be worn, and where besides, as any that *Vogue* has ever carried. His work shows, moreover, with the most poignant clarity, that it is always worth taking a risk with a young and promising artist, even if he has yet to prove himself in the subject. If he is any good at all, and given the time to work himself in, there is every chance that he will deliver.

Edward Bawden 1948
The Chelsea Flower Show

Ward withdrew as a regular contributor in the course of 1951, leaving Audrey Lewis, at that time comparatively obscure, as British *Vogue*'s sole standby. She was a charmingly straightforward illustrator in the Eric mould, professional, conventional and predictable in her work. Unassertive, and with none of Eric's conspicuous graphic flair, she nevertheless established a certain presence which was quite her own. Stemp and Bouret soon joined her, their work sympathetic in character to hers, but in both cases more dashing and overtly stylish; but already the volume of illustration used in the British, as in all the editions, was falling, and the minor names proliferated in proportion, ephemerids come and gone in a day.

In the United States there were the three stars and principals who, in their several ways, had served American *Vogue* so well over so many years, had indeed been nurtured by it, encouraged and allowed time to master its peculiar graphic disciplines. Whatever the nature or frequency of their excursions, even their lives abroad, they remained essentially the creatures of American *Vogue* for as long as their association with the magazine continued.

In the early fifties, Willaumez fell somewhat abruptly away. His contributions to the European editions had been in any case infrequent since the war, and rare indeed after 1950, though quite undiminished in their graphic authority; and soon he bowed out altogether. His work last appeared in the American edition late in 1953. Eric soldiered on, the Grand Old Man, his work as distinctively his own as ever, becoming by degrees a shade more emphatically linear, simpler and slightly less painterly. In the middle fifties he and the younger Bouché alone bestrode the three editions with anything approaching regularity; but for Eric the intervals were growing more extended and irregular, even in the American edition that had always been his principal vehicle. Forced by his last illness into comparative inactivity for a year or so, he made one late rally in a flurry of activity, and then, in the summer of 1958, he died, bringing to an end an association with *Vogue* that had lasted more than forty years. His death marked the end of the era he had seen brought in.

By 1958 René Bouché commanded the field, but was not left entirely on his own. Throughout the decade a succession of younger artists had swung along behind in support of the principals, and now for a short spell they played a larger part. Vevean, Esther Larson and Evelyn Marcil were bright, simple, confidently stylish in their work, most effectively conventional in their command of an easy, running line and the flick of the pen and brush.

And there was Dagmar, distinguished as much by her long service and consistency as by her peculiar graphic gifts. Her work for the most part was given no more prominence than the material deserved, the stock record and information that treated of collections, patterns, accessories, seasonal preoccupations. But she brought to it a lightness of touch and freedom of technique that were never less than interesting for themselves, no matter that they were

Audrey Lewis 1951

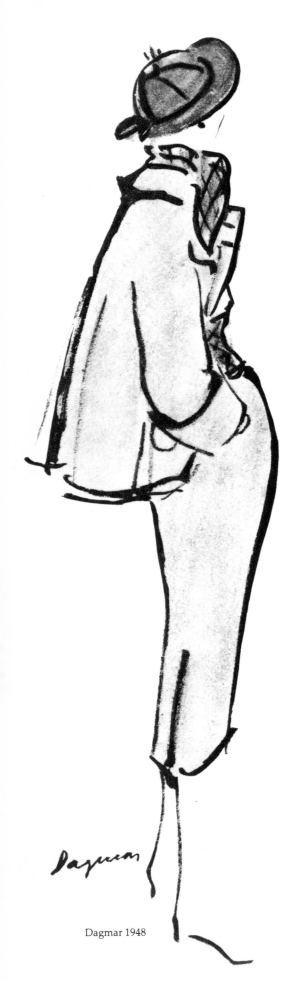

Dagmar 1948

essentially derived from other sources, in and outside the particular discipline of fashion illustration. Like some of the others, she had looked hard at Bérard, but sloughed off the exotic, heady prettiness of it all, retaining the supple and vigorous simplicity of the draughtsmanship that lay beneath. Her modesty won her the scope to develop and expand in always useful obscurity. And suddenly, in the middle and later fifties, there she was, fully fledged and a major figure if not exactly the principal. Always adventurously simple, clear-cut and direct, her work supplied a necessary astringent complement to Bouché's pervasive sweetness, and also stands as typical of *Vogue*'s last grand style of fashion illustration.

Bouché lived on a bare five years to enjoy his exposed seniority, dying suddenly in England, in July 1963, at the age of fifty-seven. No one could take his place, and indeed no one was asked to. His death seems to have marked the moment when *Vogue*'s collective heart finally set itself against the very principle of drawing to illustrate fashion. Was it perhaps coincidence; was it that a change would have come anyway, whether Bouché was there or not; or was it perhaps that his death presented at once the thought and the opportunity? Whichever it was, the facts remain that Bouché had been virtually the only illustrator employed by American *Vogue*, the only edition to employ him, since the beginning of 1963; that, though issues entirely devoid of editorial drawings were by now no means unusual, his work had been used regularly throughout his last spring and early summer; and that after his obituary appeared in the early September issue, no further fashion drawings were published by American *Vogue* that year, or indeed for a long time afterwards.

What is true of the American edition is true of them all, though the others have never been quite so rigorous in keeping drawing off their pages. There are even recent signs that drawing has been creeping back, at least in Europe, especially in the old *croquis* and sketchbook way; but there any similarity ends, for the tradition was effectively broken some twenty years ago, and all continuity of technique and discipline with it.

What followed was in no sense the fault of any decline in the quality of the graphic material admitted to the editorial pages of *Vogue*; it was the consequence of a clear change of policy. After 1963 a connection was broken for *Vogue*: there was no longer the assumption that an artist could be useful and therefore worth cultivating, whatever initial relevance his work might bear to fashion. No consideration of graphic potential was ever made again, and no Marty, Brissaud or Benito, no Eric or Willaumez, Bérard or Bouché was given an extended chance to prove himself, to demonstrate an interest and an ever more sophisticated insight or accomplishment. Drawings of course appear from time to time, but are not, except on the rarest of occasions, featured with any prominence. And on each occasion it will seem that their use has been allowed, not as a policy, but merely because it seemed a good idea at the time.

Crahay chez Lanvin, Guy Laroche,
Yves Saint-Laurent, Emanuel Ungaro 1971

Yves Saint Laurent

The drawing that does appear has changed its nature; it is now remote from the fine art tradition of direct observation and stylistic consistency that, at however distant a remove, had once informed it. It has become instead the direct product of fashion design itself, either as the mannered description of the particular designer's wares and a self-declaration of identity, or as a subsidiary or delegated activity within the fashion house or school.

Vogue is not alone in taking a direction that perhaps reflects and is yet the creature of a more general change in mood or shift of attitude; but it can hardly be anything but one of the principal examples, the monitor and mirror of its time. The sixties were indeed a curious time, when changes in the arts, and in society at large, were apparently so deeply charged with significance as to be fundamental – pregnant, it might be felt, with revolution itself. Painting appeared to be on the point of abandoning the figurative reference altogether for abstraction, and what little graphic figuration remained was increasingly committed to popular and mass-produced imagery. It is no surprise that the editors of *Vogue*, or of any magazine, should at last whole-heartedly throw in their lot with the lively and resurgent craft of the photographer.

How deceptive the New Dawn was; though a perfectly honourable proportion of the work produced in that heady time still passes muster, and the brave band of young photographers that flourished then still practise with an admirably conscientious professionalism, it is hard to say that any lasting or potent innovation was established, any epoch turned. But the rule of the camera was now absolute, and the fashion photographer became a social celebrity as he never was before, standing easy and assured in the public eye beside the rock singer and the film star. This is not to begrudge him his good fortune in touching so poignantly the contemporary nerve. It had never been quite the same for *Vogue*'s fashion artists, but they too had had their share of the fun, had been lionized in their time, the focus of current ambition for the attention in their gift

Emanuel Ungaro

Gianfranco Ferré 1982

and the power at their command to confirm or test professional and social standing. The difference lay precisely in the nature of the public that was so served, and the old days had gone for good.

The attention of those artists had always been focused upon the established order of the fashionable and elegant world, the life and celebrity of the *beau monde*; and if the other worlds of letters, politics and the creative and performing arts impinged upon that attention, their stars and personalities were registered nevertheless against the broader social and cultural backcloth. Thus it was in the work of Eric and Bouché and their colleagues, whose portraits and studies of the good and the great, the conspicuously beautiful and the currently notable or notorious, were featured so regularly by *Vogue* over so many years. Not only did the fashion artists diversify into portraiture and the passing record, but there were always with *Vogue*, if perhaps in a looser association, those artists for whom these matters were a primary concern. Cecil Beaton before the war, leaving aside his major commitment to photography, also retailed at intervals his notes and impressions of country-house life and café society at home and abroad; and, from 1939 until the early sixties, Feliks Topolski brought his own peculiar and lively vision to distinguish the pages of the magazine, keeping his own record of the twentieth century up to date with his descriptions of parades, festivals and coronations, wars and natural disasters, and his intensive studies of the faces of all manner of individuals, world leaders, great artists and philosophers.

None of that survived the sudden shift, away from the old, stabilizing, comfortable, hierarchical assumptions and social attitudes, towards the excitement and the supposed freedom of the cult of youth. The record was still to be kept, but only in photography, and it would feature rather more the heroes of youth, elevated by the mass and popular media, than the figures of Society. No longer would *Vogue* ride to hounds, and only the seasonal diversions of sea and snow would be admissible as *Vogue* sought actively to identify itself everywhere with a neutral, affluent new class.

After 1963, only one artist was commissioned by *Vogue* with any regularity at all. This was the Spanish fashion illustrator, Antonio, whose published work, over all those years, still amounts to rather less than that of Eric or Bouché, or

Antonio 1976

Lawrence Mynott 1983

indeed any of *Vogue*'s former regulars, in any normal working year. His work achieves consistency only in its stylistic variety. It is skilful, carried out with great verve, decorative and effective; yet it imposes no mood, no presence, upon the issue in which it might appear. Antonio's girls conform to the current stereotype, just as the clothes they wear, or the makeup their faces sport, conform to the current mode. This, in a certain sense, is what fashion artists have always done; but whereas Eric's stereotypes, or Pollard's, or Francis Marshall's, or Pierre Brissaud's, remain his own, Antonio appears to draw upon a more generalized stock of imagery and manner. It is well done, but adds up to an oddly impersonal declaration. It is not that Antonio is unable to keep up that old tradition to which his work could so readily lend itself, but simply that the opportunity has not been allowed him to develop his work steadily and so to assert himself. Every one of his appearances has been a kind of debut.

The point of consistency is central; without steady patronage and support, no worthwhile school of fashion illustration, as a discipline distinct in itself, is likely to revive. There will always be some fashion illustration, technical or descriptive, in the fashion schools and college departments, just as it must always be a practical and incidental function of the design studios and fashion houses. But the designer's graphic preoccupations – to draw attention to himself perhaps, or to his product, or to explain himself in technicalities to get things made – are not quite those of the artist, whose character and value have always been to see things for himself and to make his own critical evaluation.

Whether drawings and paintings will ever again be used habitually and naturally by the fashion magazine, to illustrate the functions and product of the worlds which principally concern it, is a question still unresolved. There have been signs of sorts, in the early eighties, that *Vogue*'s attention may be turning once again to the artist to supply something of its visual matter.

In September 1981, Fernando Botero, in *Vogue*'s own words 'the celebrated Colombian painter', was invited by the French edition to illustrate that autumn's collection. This, in a magnificent sequence of fifteen paintings and a dozen drawings, he proceeded to do, and yet without compromising himself or modifying his work to the slightest degree. His obsessively, emphatically bulbous and wholly delightful ladies, who confound so spectacularly the conventional wisdom of our times that the fat can never be beautiful, let alone most elegantly fashionable, show off the creations of the great Paris houses, the very highest of high fashion, as never before. Botero's extraordinary fashion plates are manifestly sympathetic and charming, witty and sometimes very funny besides; but chiefly they are demonstrably practical and effective.

This is not to say that Señor Botero should for ever after earn his living in the *salons* and studios of the Parisian Couture; but the simple point is that, having been asked, he performed with a notable and evidently repeatable professionalism, to exquisite effect. As it was for Botero, so it could be for other

Zoltan 1982 >

174

artists of similar competence and subjective interest; but, fun though the occasional treat or surprise undoubtedly is, there would seem to be little point in such arbitrary pleasures, indulged as they now are in isolation. For artists are practical and serious people, and their work feeds on itself, growing and developing, changing and modifying as the practice continues. To fail in the particular case to allow such development to take place, for interest, knowledge and expertise to grow together, is to deny an audience unnecessarily the experience, in contemporary terms, of an applied, peculiar and honourable discipline of the visual arts.

Drawing is not photography, its product neither mechanical, unselective nor predictable, its point never the total recall of particular reference or information, but always the image refined, simplified and ordered through an individual sensibility. It is as old a process and discipline as civilization itself, as natural and sophisticated a means of fixing experience as it is a vehicle of information or expression, and ever capable of surprise and delight to the informed and sympathetic eye.

Fernando Botero 1981

A quick look over her shoulder, and off she steps, with perhaps just a shade of apprehension across her nervous, pretty face, into the brave new post-war world; but none of the problems of 1947 need really concern Eric's young lady at just this minute, with so much else on her mind. 'You know it the minute you see it: that a red hat is the find of the season . . . You know it the minute you wear one: that its strength is as the strength of ten, when it comes to making memorable effect. . . . You'll know it as the season progresses: that red can be dangerous in too large doses.'

A rapid notation was still the chief convention of drawing in *Vogue*. That rapidity, however, is deceptive: Eric, apparently so free in hand and eye, was known to take endless pains, imposing agonies of immobility on his models, and who can say that *Vogue*'s other artists were any quicker? But how lively and effective that final refinement is: here Willaumez's proud American lady (left, 1949) steps out in narrow black Balenciaga, or (below, 1948) in a tweed stole that is no longer mere 'extra wrapping to wear now and then over this or that'. Tom Keogh in France (right, 1949) finds Balenciaga again and *La Mode du Soir*, all stately satin, mousseline charm and décolletage.

Surrealism has informed *Vogue* since the early thirties, both in the work invited from such distinguished artists as Giorgio de Chirico, Salvador Dalí, Pavel Tchelitchew and Pierre Roy, and in the work of such house artists and

photographers as Cecil Beaton, Erwin Blumenfeld and, of course, Bérard. After the war, Coltellacci marked French *Vogue* with his idiosyncratic and theatrical variety. Here (1947), a bizarre *commedia dell'arte* troupe performing at the edge of the world. Le Cirque du Printemps (left), and a satin shirt and taffeta dress from Balmain. And from Balenciaga (right), Vanity Fair – a grand caped evening cloak and a long straight gown.

Vertès

Drawing as social observation, or social observation as the pretext for spreading the fashion word: either way, horsy people in horsy places, doing horsy things, are just the sort to point the pencil at. Vertès (left and below, 1948) is in New York for 'The Ziegfeld Follies of the horse world', the National Horse Show in Madison Square Garden. Eric (right, 1948) is off to the races, where, as is so well known, 'Women owners are modest in their betting, shrewd in their buying, sentimental about their racing colours.' And the clothes for those racing places: 'Nothing in the world "collects" a bland colour like black.'

Tom Keogh enlivened the pages mostly of French *Vogue* for too brief a spell. Here he is, typically with a splash of strong colour, an uncompromising silhouette and a swift line. He has a sweeter delicacy than even Bérard at his most romantic; but now he is closer to the graphic sweep and confidence of Eric or Willaumez. He reflects a new spirit, too – a flatter colour and simplified outline that affected many *Vogue* artists, especially Gruau, in the fifties. Yet in all his moods Keogh is unmistakably himself: here a mauve draped overcoat by Mad Carpentier (right, 1948); and, by Jeanne Lanvin (centre, 1950), full, swinging velvet and a flash of lining, and with it a strapless gown by Balmain pulled close around hips and seat.

The social round whirls on, from Henley at the height of the summer season to the grandest of autumn balls; and that seductive movement is caught and fixed for us here in 1950 by John Ward, one of the most naturally gifted draughtsmen ever employed by *Vogue* – delicate, informative, restrained. But his eye and hand were so very English that he remained British *Vogue*'s alone to enjoy, and only for a few short years. For the ball, bare shoulders, and a fan-like corsage and bouffant-satin gown, or a hipped and bowed extravaganzà in orchid brocade. For Henley, a white jacket-dress and coolie beret, worn straight and flat.

Bouché by now is firmly established as one of *Vogue*'s principals and frequently holds the centre of the stage, waiting only for Eric or Willaumez to step aside. Though he shares with Willaumez a love of sharp and acid colour, and at times an almost frantic calligraphy in his drawing, his mood is always softer; it is always to Eric that his work bears the closest relation. Seldom, however, are they so close as this, as to be almost in each other's shoes. In 1948 in America, Eric (left) has the news from Paris and Schiaparelli, 'The sharply angled silhouette . . . the spiral flounces wired to wing out. Above the excitement, the high severity of black silk jersey; and Bouché (right), 'This Autumn . . . twice as appealing to the colour-loving masculine eye . . . Try a red suit.'

Audrey Lewis's delicate descriptive drawings appeared in British *Vogue* for many years (above, 1950); Eric Stemp, another British regular, was rather more assertive a presence, with an authentic whiff of period (far right, 1955). More confident still were the rare contributions of Brian, mostly in American or, as here, in French *Vogue* (near right, 1953).

In 1950 in American *Vogue* Count Willaumez is still in his pomp, as impressive as ever, effortlessly commanding the generous space he is still given with his dramatic image of Woman as the chic ideal, always in the highest, the latest fashion, the very picture of transatlantic elegance. Here (left), a eucalyptus-green taffeta dress, and a matador jacket dotted with jet beads, by Adrian: and (right) from Hattie Carnegie's ready-to-wear collection, 'a ball dress of sea-grey silk satin'.

René Gruau appeared just after the war, and is still at work in the early eighties. His contribution has always been more to the advertising than the editorial pages, but here in 1954 (left), when his mature manner is firmly established, is a typically emphatic image of a Balenciaga linen suit, with strong tonality and clear silhouette, and the spattered background, flicked on no doubt with a toothbrush, recalling the texture of a poster by Lautrec. Other illustrators come and go – and Vevean's ambivalent signature is subscribed to some of American *Vogue*'s most lively and expressive drawings of the middle fifties: these (right) are from 1955.

Eric was part of *Vogue* for more than thirty-five years. His drawing, in *Vogue*'s own words, was 'to the Paris couture . . . the most desired of representations for their designs'. He died in 1958, at the age of sixty-seven, after an illness that over his last few months had prevented him from working with his habitual regularity. This drawing (far left) is of 1957, and Eric is his old, so relaxedly elegant self. This leaves Bouché, last of the old school, to carry the flag for another year or two (left, 1960); and indeed it is not too fanciful to detect on these two pages the natural graphic sympathy between them, and in Eric's gentleman a line that might well have been Bouché's own.

For many years there was always room for the drawn portrait in *Vogue*, and within the scope of *Vogue*'s spotlight almost any fashionable subject would do – theatre, society, films, the arts, fashion itself. Here *Vogue* could show the creative, the distinguished and the great – and, if they happened to be men, well, *Vogue* had never considered itself to be solely a women's magazine. In time almost all the regular contributors had a go: here, by Gruau (far left, 1962), the Italian couturier, Emilio Pucci; by Bouché (left, 1956), the young Sammy Davis Jr., 'a meagre, sharp fellow, crammed with talent'; and again by Bouché (right, 1960), Walter Pidgeon, sometime romantic Hollywood lead, but now somewhat older and starring on Broadway.

There has always been a place in *Vogue* for exotic travel. Bouché went to Japan in 1957 and in a luscious and detailed feature reported back on the two-hour make-up ritual of Toyosuro, maiko of the Pontocho geisha quarter of Kyoto. As intimately privileged as Toulouse-Lautrec or Degas in the dressing-rooms of Montmartre, Bouché found there, he says: 'a world of femininity of which we have no idea', and which hardly exists outside this section of the old capital. The life of Toyosura, still in her apprenticeship, conforms to the old way: up at ten, lessons until midday, rehearsals or shopping until three, when she must begin this ritual preparation; and then from six until dawn the arduous succession of engagements at which 'she must make one party after another enjoyable for her guests through her skill . . . in the traditional geisha arts'.

The star artists of course held the centre of the stage; their eminence was sustained by a succession of more modest but nevertheless most useful artists, those steadies who served the magazine with such admirable consistency and reliability over so many years, for just so long as *Vogue* chose to enjoy their services. The three who are seen here, though distinct and particular in themselves, are typical of the final, established graphic style that obtained until the death of Bouché in 1963, when quite suddenly illustration was all but banished from the pages of the magazine. Bouret (far left, 1957), with an Irish linen suit that 'might contribute as much figure-flattery as a reducing treatment', served all three editions for more than a decade. Hervé Dubly, whose work for the most part was confined to French *Vogue*, shows a flurry of pleats and taffeta chiffon (left, 1959). Esther Larson, seen only in American *Vogue*, draws the 'torsolette' (right, 1963), with its 'soft, high-lifting lace brassiere above . . . a small but unpinching waist'.

Dagmar, getting simpler, bolder, ever more forceful in her later work for *Vogue*, and winning in consequence much more prominence for her work (left, 1961); and Evelyn Marcil, by no means so long-serving, but in the few years around 1960 fully deserving every chance to show off her elegantly animated and sketchy young ladies (right, 1960; far right, 1961). Fresh, clean and simple colour, strong, uncomplicated line, and the clearest of silhouettes, characterize the work of both artists; but Dagmar is always the more adventurous, the more consciously modern. Evelyn Marcil is less ambitious, but graphically most sophisticated.

The good and the great and the beautiful continue to appear, as they always have in the pages of *Vogue*. Here, by Bouché, America's First Lady of the moment (1961), Mrs John Kennedy, winner of *Vogue*'s own talent contest ten years before: 'a straight-out beauty with three extra qualities, brains, gentleness and charm'. Also by Bouché, the doyenne of England's Americans, Nancy Astor. And from Feliks Topolski (1960), already a regular and distinguished contributor for more than twenty years, whose particular gift remains his idiosyncratic eye for great events and the people who inform them, characteristic images of a keeper of society's conscience, Bertrand, The Earl Russell, and of an acute observer of its follies, Evelyn Waugh.

René Bouché's work continued to appear principally in American *Vogue*, as regular, graceful and evocative as ever, until his death in 1963. And with his going, a habit in *Vogue* died too: the assumption that drawing, the natural complement to photography, had its rightful place in *Vogue*'s scheme of things. Quite suddenly the door was closed, to be opened in the future only by occasional invitation. The artists drifted away, no longer sustained by consistent employment and the opportunity it affords to develop and mature the work, month by month, year by year, in this special and exacting discipline. These two illustrations of Bouché (left, 1961; right, 1962) are splendid and entirely characteristic images.

Like others before him, Tod Draz, recruited from the advertising pages, enlivened the editorial content for a brief spell, though only in the French and British editions. At the very end of what might be called the age of illustration, his vigorous and confident work stands as the very type of that freely expressive grand style passed down through Bouché and Eric from the masters of the École de Paris. Above and right are a Givenchy hat of 1960 and Balenciaga's raglan coat of 1961. There was, however, a long midsummer twilight, extending even into the middle sixties with such drawings as Barbara Pearlman's consciously emphatic description of the flounces and pleats of the evening mode, if it could now bear so formal a designation, of 1965 – a time when drawing of any kind was an unlooked-for variant and treat.

Of all the latter-day artists whom *Vogue*, in the European editions at least, has chosen to employ, Antonio has been the most frequent visitor, and still appears with a certain regularity. He has proved himself as versatile and various as ever Benito was, though perhaps rather more self-consciously assertive. In 1970 (left), by no means his first appearance, he is characteristically different and decorative – fey and flower-power with a long and willowy knife-pleated outfit by Bill Gibb: 'Grass roots is the mood for this summer, and the look is handwoven, handpainted, handknitted, handstitched.' This was the mood, too, one supposes, for Urs Landis earlier in the same year (right), though his was only a Beauty Feature for the French edition, and the one chance *Vogue* ever gave him to prove himself. And is it Antonio's direct influence we see in this strongly drawn yet so conventionally pretty picture, or does it reflect a more general spirit of the time? And is there too, perhaps, just a nod of acknowledgment to Bouché?

The pattern of occasional graphic indulgence is set; and how decorative and pleasing it can be – Philippe Caron here, in French *Vogue* (left, 1965), enjoying to the full delicious French underwear at its most Frenchly delicious. And as the artists give way, the designers move in, with fashion drawing by now so much more the natural product of the designer's than of the artist's studio: here 'Pablo & Delia Draw Grown-Ups – design new clothes to look like this' (right, 1972).

Antonio rings the changes upon the close-up image of the face and woman's urge to make it up; and swings from a Fauve directness (right, 1973; near left above, 1974) to subtle and more contemporary references to collage, and such artists as Richard Hamilton and Andy Warhol (far left above, 1981; far left below, 1980; near left below, 1980).

As powerful and memorable a set of drawings as any in the entire canon, and all the more so for coming so late in the day, so shockingly lonely and so wonderfully direct. All *Vogue* artists have drawn what amounts to the nude, but seldom with such manifest relish: Antonio draws 'Paloma Picasso wearing the new halter bras' (1972).

Still it seems a very good idea to invite an artist of some real distinction and achievement in the wider creative world beyond couture and the mode to concern himself for once, as much for his own enjoyment as for professional advancement or commercial ploy, with the peculiar and ephemeral minutiae of this minute's highest fashion. French *Vogue* is prepared to take the plunge, at least now and again; and Fernando Botero, *'le célèbre peintre colombien'*, and his bulbous ladies, confound whatever doubts may have been entertained as to the wisdom of the enterprise. These wonderful images, two only from a portfolio of fifteen paintings and twelve drawings, are as descriptive and effective as they are hugely enjoyable: coat on coat and true Scotch plaid, the trousers lined and turned with silk to match the blouse, by Nina Ricci; and from Chanel, the very newest and most ample of double-breasted tweed overcoats (1981).

A stylish debut, and a guest reappearance or two (all in 1978) for Harvey Boyd in the hospitable pages of French *Vogue*. His energetic and forceful drawing, though so unmistakably late-seventies, spirited and mocking, is also oddly redolent of the work of *Vogue*'s artists a generation before, freely drawn, decorative, and yet none the less informative – shades perhaps of early Bouché, or of Tod Draz or Hervé Dubly a little later on.

René Gruau (1981) is clearly as fond of
strong silhouette, and stronger
chiaroscuro, as ever: short draped taffeta
dress from Yves Saint Laurent, that
finishes with two frills and a large 'pouf'
at the side – *mot dernier* indeed.

Postscript

The great mass of my research was direct into the pages of *Vogue* itself, in the volumes of its American, British and French editions as they were available to me in *Vogue*'s own library in London. My intention in presenting this material from *Vogue* alone, was simply to open up the subject once more, to show the curious, the interested and the forgetful just how rich a field this was, and so recently. If it remains wide open, so much more welcome are others to walk in: and if the suggestion takes, that artists might be encouraged again to editorial advantage and public delight, so much the better.

I do add a short list of authorities whom I found myself all too glad to consult:

Always In Vogue – Edna Woolman Chase & Ilka Chase: Victor Gollancz 1954
The Man Who Was Vogue – Caroline Seebohm: Viking Press 1982
The Changing World of Fashion – Ernestine Carter: Weidenfeld & Nicolson 1977
Paris in the Third Reich – David Pryce-Jones: Collins 1981
A Fashion of Life – H. W. Yoxall: Heinemann 1966

'The Muse and Vertès'

Acknowledgments

This book could not have been made without the active help of many people, and the generous encouragement of very many more: but in particular I owe an unrepayable debt of gratitude to the staff of *Vogue*'s Book Department in London – to Elizabeth Prior, Charlie Lee-Potter, Jane Mulvagh and Anna Houghton, not one of whom ever failed to answer a cry for help, however faint or trivial – to Christina Probert, who was ever free with the favour of her deep and special knowledge of Fashion, its history and practice – to Bunny Cantor, who uncomplainingly allowed me, even helped me at times, to disrupt the smooth order of her library, often for weeks on end – and to Alex Kroll, the General Editor of Condé Nast Books, who was with the project from the very first, always wholeheartedly enthusiastic, and confident of its success.

William Packer

Nos Artistes Américains à Paris et à Londres

Things that interest me.

Catharine Hopkins

CATHARINE HOPKINS
PARIS

Ah Paris! To interpret your chic, movement, smartness in all its complicated simplicity, and elegance, and sometimes even to find a combination of beauty and real feeling.
Porter Woodruff.

PORTER WOODRUFF
PARIS

CARL ERICKSON
PARIS

After Vogue drawings my principal pre-occupation is keeping in my shell
Polly Francis

POLLY TIGHE FRANCIS
PARIS

LEE CREELMAN
PARIS

Good heavens is that what he looks like!

FREDERICK C. CHAPMAN
LONDRES

GEORGE W. PLANK
LONDRES

Little Twitts Cottage.
Five Ashes.
Sussex.

Dearest Vogue:
My emotions are beyond any expressing — what CAN I say? — We have been happily married for more than eleven years and I (literally) could not live without you! All blessings, admiration and constant affection from your devoted
George Plank.

Nos Artistes à New York

I love all animals except spiders and some people
Claire Avery —

CLAIRE AVERY

JEAN OLIVER

OLGA THOMAS WAGSTAFF

A la Re —
The country —
Sincerity —
To laugh —
Simplicity —
To read —
Paris —
old furniture —
The primitive Italian painters —
Beautiful clothes —
The history of France —
Good architecture —
The last Publications —
To travel —
Out door sports —
work —
Helen Dryden —

HELEN DRYDEN

LESLIE SAALBURG

ROBERT E. LOCHER

JOHN MORDECAI
BARBOUR

I like — simplicity in all things and people. I hate prettiness and ice cream. I also like being one of the younger artists.
Harriet Meserole

HARRIET MESEROLE

DOUGLAS POLLARD   E. B. HERRICK

IRMA CAMPBELL

A spread from French *Vogue*, March 1923

Nos Artistes Français

PIERRE MOURGUE

ANDRÉ MARTY

...ET DE PROFIL:

GEORGES LEPAPE

CHARLES MARTIN

MARIO SIMON

EDOUARD-GARCIA BENITO

CHARLES MARTIN

BERNARD BOUTET DE MONVEL

ANDRÉ MARTY

PIERRE BRISSAUD

A spread from French *Vogue*, March 1923

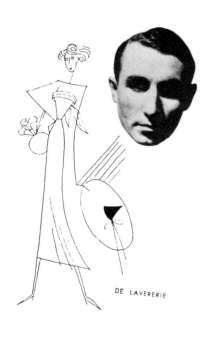

DE LAVERERIE

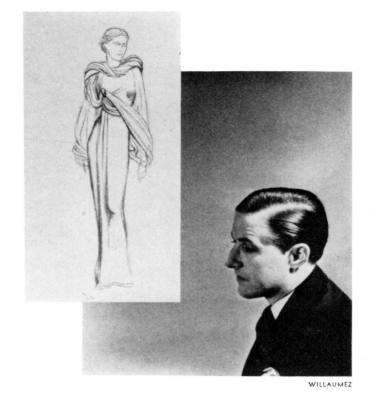

WILLAUMEZ

PORTER WOODRUFF

BENITO

LIBISZEWSKI

POLLY TIGHE FRANCIS

BOLIN

'Several times, we have caught our artists making furtive little sketches on the sides of the paper destined for a fashion drawing. On closer inspection, the sketches proved to be a sort of wish-fulfilment: wistful conceptions of what they would have liked to draw instead of what they were supposed to draw; women clothed in garments closer to the artist's thwarted ideal. Seeing this, we thought we'd drag their ideas into the light of day; and, as a form of midsummer levity, present them to you.

'We were amused to see how true each artist was to type – and how fundamentally conservative. Somehow, we expected dire revelations. But, they show little desire to revolutionize the feminine façade.'

(From American *Vogue*, 1 August 1933.)

PIERRE MOURGUE

RUTH SIGRID GRAFSTROM

THE DAVID TWINS

LEE CREELMAN ERICKSON

CARL ERICKSON

GEORGES LEPAPE

JEAN PAGÈS

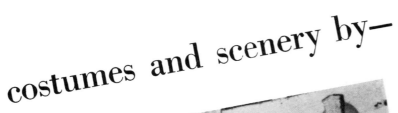

Christian Bérard

Cecil Beaton

'Ever since the walls of Jericho fell there have been occasions when a blowing of trumpets seemed indicated. And here, we think, is one of them. For these three young men, well in the limelight as stage designers, are also Vogue artists, and in our pages frequently bend their talents to presenting modes and manners.

'**Cecil Beaton** appears here in the rôle of stage designer – he works for Cochran's revues, *Apparitions* and *Le Pavillon* then at Covent Garden; but people who can do anything can do everything it seems, so one takes for granted his versatility in drawing, photographing and writing for Vogue as well. This is how he describes his career: "My earliest photographs were of my sisters, then about five and six years old, and were taken with a small box Brownie against a sheet hung up in the garden, in imitation of the professional photographs of the beauties of the day – Lily Elsie and Diana Cooper. Generally the results were out of focus. Later, I bought a 3a Kodak and an artificial lamp. Hence without pre-planning I became a photographer, but it was as draughtsman that I first worked for Vogue. Mrs. Fellowes liked my spidery efforts, explaining that they looked as though I was trying to do them as badly as I could. In my stage experience work for the Russian Ballet is like working for monkeys – each dancer destroys the costume if possible, and I have to leave fierce and ruthless instructions for the carrying out of my designs".'

234

Marcel Vertès at Alick Johnstone's studio

'**Christian Bérard** is a true Bohemian – impulsive, unpunctual, untidy, and apt to sit all night at a café in passionate discussion of art. Pity he shaved that beard. Bérard, who comes of a long line of distinguished architects, soon justified his break-away from the family profession by becoming one of the leaders of the young French school. He has painted fine portraits, designed unforgettable stage settings – for *La Machine Infernale*, *L'Ecole des Femmes*, *Margot*, *Cotillon*, and finally in *Symphonie Fantastique* brought off one of the major sensations of the season by his marvellous colour and his power of capturing atmosphere, whether of beauty or of dreadfulness. (Scene 3 of the ballet appears in skeleton surrealist fashion across his chest.) Like so many modern artists he has a passion for interior decorating – regarding a house as a larger kind of canvas. Sufficient proof of his gifts that he has decorated the houses of such famous professionals as Jean-Michel Frank and Syrie Maugham. He also sits at the source of fashion.

'**Marcel Vertès** tell us: "I was born not so very long ago in Hungary. They intended me for a lawyer, but I felt my vocation was to design aeroplanes. One day my pretty young sister met me. My boiler suit reeked with oil, my bruised hands were black with grease. She burst into tears, and confessed she dreamed of a different lot for her brother. 'Be an artist,' she begged, quoting from favourite novels' descriptions of studios: animal skins on divans, mandolins on the walls. As a final argument she added, lowering her eyes, that artists painted women in the nude. I was tempted, and with the help of my elder sister Dola (I owe everything to women) I left for Paris where I attempt to live up to my sister's dreams for me." He has succeeded. There is both satire and beauty in his series of illustrated books on his favourite subject, "woman," and in his décor for revues in Paris, Charity Balls in New York, and now of *Transatlantic Rhythm* in London. He illustrates Colette, Zola, Morand, draws fashion for *Vogue* and tosses off articles.'

A spread from British *Vogue*, September 1936

235

From American *Vogue*, 15 March 1947. Artists: Willaumez, Eric, Bouché. Photographer: Penn

John Ward

Sources of illustrations

The abbreviations AV, BV, FV, and GV stand for American Vogue, British Vogue, French Vogue and German Vogue. Drawings were frequently used in more than one edition, and the editions acknowledged here are not necessarily those in which they appeared originally. The figures (1) and (2) indicate the first and second issue in a month.

1 Ann Fish BV May (1) 1920
2 René Bouché AV Sep. (1) 1949
4 Eric BV May 1957

Introduction (pp. 8–32)

8 Meidias, *Dancing Maenad*, red-figure hydria, 5th century BC
9 (above) Hans Holbein, *Cecily Heron*, 1526–28. Reproduced by gracious permission of Her Majesty the Queen.
9 (below) Wenceslaus Hollar, *Muffs and Lace*, 1647. British Museum (Dept of Prints and Drawings), London
10 Benito AV Apr. (2) 1921
11 Marty AV Aug. (2) 1922
12 George Plank AV Mar. (1) 1927
13 Mario Simon AV Mar. (2) 1922
14 Eric FV Sep. 1929
15 Eric AV Aug. (1) 1946
16 Eric AV Feb. (1) 1947
17 John Ward BV Mar. 1949
18 (above left) Helen Dryden AV Sep. (2) 1926
18 (below left) Edgar Degas, *Mary Cassatt at the Louvre*, c.1880. Henry P. McIlhenny Collection, Philadelphia
18 (below right) Paul-César Helleu, *Madame Helleu*, 1895–1900.
19 René Bouché AV Mar. (1) 1948
20 (left) Tom Keogh FV Apr. 1948
20 (above right) Henri de Toulouse-Lautrec, *Le Divan Japonais*, 1892. Victoria and Albert Museum, London
20 (below right) Marcel Vertès AV Apr. (2) 1953
21 René Gruau AV Oct. (2) 1949
22 (above left) Aubrey Beardsley, *The Black Cape*, 1894 (illustration for Oscar Wilde's play *Salome*)
22 (below left) Léonard Foujita AV Jan. (2) 1931
22 (right) Kwaigetsude Anchi (Chogodo), *A Beauty of the Day*, c.1710–20. British Museum, London.

23 Helen Dryden AV Jan. (1) 1923
24 (above left) Henri Matisse, *Les Yeux Bleus*, 1935. Baltimore Museum of Art, Cone Collection
(below left) Kees van Dongen AV Dec. (2) 1926
(below right) Christian Bérard BV 22 Dec. 1937
25 Eric AV Jun. (2) 1932
26 Salvador Dalí AV Nov. (1) 1949
27 (left) Coltellacci AV Jan. (1) 1944
(above right) Giorgio de Chirico AV Jan. (1) 1937
(below right) Benito AV Oct. (1) 1939
28 (above left) Salvador Dalí AV Jun. (1) 1939
(below left) Pierre Roy AV Apr. (1) 1938
(right) Amedeo Modigliani, *Head with an Abacus*, 1911–12. Private collection
29 Benito BV 2 Oct. 1929
30 Andy Warhol AV May 1977
31 (above) Richard Hamilton BV 15 Mar. 1970
(below) Antonio BV Aug. 1970
32 David Hockney BV 1 Mar. 1973

Part One (pp. 33–96)

33 John Barbour BV Nov. (1) 1924
34 Paul Iribe AV Jun. (2) 1920
35 (above) Bernard Boutet de Monvel AV Dec. (1) 1922
(below) George Barbier AV May (1) 1919
36 (above) Pierre Brissaud, Georges Lepape, André Marty BV 1 Aug. 1922
(centre) Pierre Brissaud AV Jan. (1) 1923
(below) André Marty AV Jan. (1) 1923
37 (above) Charles Martin AV Jan. (1) 1923
(centre) Mario Simon AV Jan. (1) 1923
(below) Mario Simon, Benito, Charles Martin BV 1 Aug. 1922
38 (above) Benito BV Sep. (2) 1924
(below) Pierre Brissaud FV 1 Jan. 1923
39 Pierre Brissaud AV Feb. (1) 1931
40 (above) Olga Thomas Wagstaff AV Jul. (1) 1920
(below) Irma Campbell AV Dec. (2) 1922 .
41 (above) Claire Avery AV Jul. (2) 1920

(below) E. B. Herrick AV Aug. (1) 1920
42 Pierre Mourgue AV Sep. (2) 1930
43 Lee Creelman Erickson AV Dec. (2) 1925
44 (above) Ann Fish AV Feb. (2) 1921
(below) Mark Ogilvie-Grant BV 11 Jul. 1928
45 (above) Libis BV 11 Jan. 1928
(below) Roger de Lavererie FV Dec. 1929
46 (above) Joseph Platt BV Aug. (1) 1925
(below) Lambarri BV 22 Feb. 1928
47 Francis Marshall BV 11 Dec. 1929
48 René Bouët-Willaumez BV 1 Apr. 1931
49 Georges Lepape AV Jan. (1) 1923
50 André Marty BV 2 Apr. 1923
51 (left) Porter Woodruff AV Jan. (1) 1924
(right) Benito BV Apr. (2) 1923
52 Mario Simon BV 1 Jan. 1923
53 (above) Benito BV 1 Jan. 1923
(below) Pierre Brissaud AV Jul. (1) 1922
(below right) André Marty AV Nov. (2) 1924
54 (above) André Marty BV Jul. (1) 1923
(below) Pierre Brissaud FV Aug. 1923
55 André Marty BV Jul. (1) 1923
56 (above left) Porter Woodruff AV Mar. (1) 1924
(above right) Polly Francis FV May 1924
(below left) Robert Locher FV 1 Feb. 1924
57 (above) Charles Martin FV 1 May 1924
(below right) Guillermo Bolín BV Apr. (1) 1925
58 Harriet Meserole AV Apr. (1) 1924
59 Harriet Meserole AV Jul. (1) 1924
60 (left) Benito AV Nov. (2) 1924
(right) Kees van Dongen AV Oct. (2) 1926
61 Jean Dupas AV Feb. (1) 1925
62 Benito BV 2 Dec. 1924
63 (above left) Mario Simon AV Feb. (1) 1924
(above right) Polly Francis FV Sep. 1925
(below right) Benito AV Jun. (2) 1924
64 (left) Benito BV Aug. (2) 1926
(right) Lee Creelman Erickson AV Aug. (1) 1927
65 André Marty FV Mar. 1928
66 Porter Woodruff AV Feb. (1) 1926

67 (left) Porter Woodruff AV Apr. (1) 1926
(right) Benito BV Feb. (2) 1925
68 Ernst Dryden FV Apr. 1928
69 Georges Lepape BV Mar. (2) 1926
70 Bernard Boutet de Monvel BV 2 Mar. 1925
71 (above) Harriet Meserole AV Jun. (1) 1926
(right) Leslie Saalburg AV Oct. (1) 1925
72 Eric AV Apr. (2) 1929
73 Jean Pagès AV May (2) 1931
74 Pierre Brissaud AV Jun. (1) 1925
75 (above left) L. Fellows BV 2 Nov. 1927
(above right) Leslie Saalburg AV Mar. (2) 1929
(below) Guillermo Bolín AV Mar. (1) 1926
76, 77 Jean Pagès AV Mar. (1) 1931
78 (above left) Douglas Pollard AV Mar. (1) 1926
(above right) Douglas Pollard BV Oct. (2) 1926
(below) Douglas Pollard FV Mar. 1933
79 Douglas Pollard BV Mar. (1) 1927
80 Guillermo Bolín AV Feb. (2) 1931
81 Eric AV Nov. (2) 1932
82 (above left and below left) Francis Marshall BV 30 Sep. 1936
82–83 Jean Pagès AV Jan. (2) 1932
83 (above right and below right) Francis Marshall BV 30 Sep. 1936
84, 85 Pierre Mourgue AV Jan. (1) 1934
86 (left) Eric FV Aug. 1934
86 (right) Pierre Mourgue AV Dec. (1) 1933
87 Pierre Mourgue FV Dec. 1934
88 Ruth Grafstrom AV Feb. (2) 1933
89 Eric AV Mar. (2) 1933
90 (left) René Bouët-Willaumez AV Sep. (1) 1933
(right) René Bouët-Willaumez BV 5 Sep. 1934
91 Eric BV 7 Mar. 1934
92 René Bouët-Willaumez AV Sep. (1) 1934
93 Eric BV 27 Jun. 1934
94 (above) Cecil Beaton BV 20 Sep. 1933
(below left) Cecil Beaton BV 2 Oct. 1929
(below right) Cecil Beaton BV 4 Apr. 1928
95 Cecil Beaton BV 21 Mar. 1934
96 René Bouët-Willaumez AV Feb. (1) 1934

Index *of artists, movements, designers, editors*

Oodles to Do with Loo-Loo and Boo
The Collected Art Adventures

Dear Parents,

Because your children are so amazingly smart and talented, they'll have fun doing these step-by-step art projects. You don't have to buy any fancy materials and the only thing that could possibly be of danger in this book is your child's own imagination. You can do art with your children — if they invite you — but please don't do their art for them. If you're tempted to borrow this book and use it, we suggest you do it while your children are asleep and please put it back in the morning.

**Love,
Mrs. Loo-Loo and Mrs. Boo**

Compilation copyright © 2001 by Denis Roche
Part one from *Loo-Loo, Boo, and Art You Can Do,* Copyright © 1996 by Denis Roche
Part two from *Art Around the World: Loo-Loo, Boo, and More Art You Can Do,*
Copyright © 1998 by Denis Roche

www.houghtonmifflinbooks.com

ISBN 0-618-15423-X

Library of Congress Control Number: 2001130387

Manufactured in Singapore
TWP 10 9 8 7 6 5 4 3 2 1

Oodles to Do with Loo-Loo and Boo
The Collected Art Adventures
by Denis Roche

Houghton Mifflin Company
Boston 2001

For Jane, Kevin, and Ursula,
three of the best artists I know,
and for Paud, who sticks like glue

Tables of Content

Stuff We Need To Tell You Before You Begin

You might want to wear a smock when you paint or do other messy projects. Get an old T-shirt or shirt from your parent and wear that. Some people like to wear their smocks backward so that paint and goo doesn't fall through the buttonholes. Don't forget to roll up your sleeves!

You can do any project on the floor or on a table. Usually it is a good idea to lay down newspapers before you start. Water jars and paint almost always tip over, and it's easier to clean up if you've put down newspapers. You can tape the newspapers down to make them less slippery.

Help!

What kind of glue should you use? Glue sticks are OK for paper, but we think white liquid glue works best for the projects in this book.

You're so strong!

There are two kinds of paint you can use. Watercolor paint is a thin paint. It shows up best on white paper. Watercolor paint will have <u>more</u> color if you use <u>less</u> water.

Poster paint is also called tempera paint. This paint is very thick and lots of fun to use. Poster paint is good for mixing new colors or working on cardboard. It usually doesn't wash out of clothing.

If your paint came in big jars, it is easier to use and share if you pour smaller amounts into an empty egg carton. You can use the extra spaces in the carton to mix new colors. Some people like to use plates (paper or real) to mix colors too.

While you're painting, you need a water jar so you can clean your brush every time you change colors. Use a bigger water jar for bigger brushes and change your water when it gets really yucky. When you're finished painting, wash your brushes in the sink until all the paint stuck on them goes down the drain.

Potato Prints

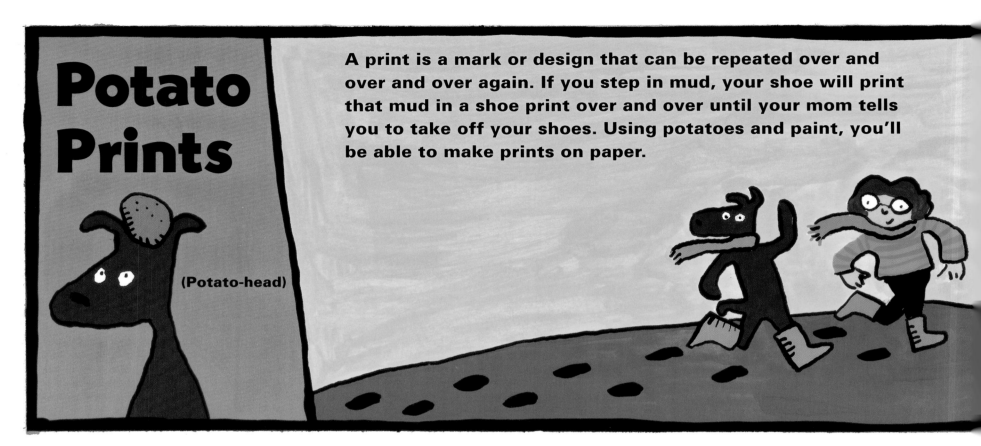

(Potato-head)

A print is a mark or design that can be repeated over and over and over again. If you step in mud, your shoe will print that mud in a shoe print over and over until your mom tells you to take off your shoes. Using potatoes and paint, you'll be able to make prints on paper.

Ask your parents for whole, uncooked potatoes. They probably keep them in the kitchen.

Cut the potatoes in half with a plastic knife, then put the flat part of the potato on the table.

Now here comes the tricky part.

(But any potato-head can do it.)

Looking down at your potato half, you see a circle. You need to cut the edges off the potato to make different shapes.

Can you make a square? Using your knife, cut off pieces of the circle to make one.

A star?

What other shapes can you make?

Now you're going to print. Pour poster paint onto a plate. Press the face of the potato into the paint, then press it down on a piece of paper. You can print more than one time before you need to dip the potato back into the paint again.

When you're finished printing and waiting for the paint to dry, try balancing a whole potato on your head.

Sculptures

Have you ever pretended that you were a statue? A statue is a sculpture. A sculpture is a piece of art that has more than one side. A sculpture is never flat.

To make your sculpture you'll need:

a flat piece of cardboard

empty cans

empty milk cartons

cardboard tubes

any kind of boxes

glue

Where do you get cardboard tubes? From paper towels and toilet paper, of course. But wait until the paper is finished before you use them!

Wash any dirty cans or cartons.

What you decide to build can look like anything or nothing at all. Sometimes the shape of your cans and cartons will give you ideas.

Use the flat piece of cardboard as a base for your sculpture. Build up from the piece of cardboard, using the cans, milk cartons, and tubes, gluing them together as you go along.

When you're done building, you can paint or decorate your sculpture.

Bumpy Paint

It's important for roads to be flat.

And flat toast is a good idea too, because then you can spread stuff on it easily.

But do paintings have to be flat?

There's really no good reason.

Here's a way to make a bumpy painting.

You'll need:

sand

empty cans or jars

poster paint

glue

big paintbrushes

paper

14

Put some sand into each of your cans or jars.

Now pour the same amount of paint into each one.

Add a big squirt of glue to each jar.

With big paintbrushes, stir the mixtures until they're as thick as milk shakes.

It's going to feel different painting with bumpy paint. You smush it onto the paper instead of smoothing it on.

When you're finished painting and ready to clean up, do not put any paint down the sink. Throw it in the trash instead, and wash your brushes extra well.

Stinky Clay

There are lots of things you can make with clay, and even more things to make if you change your mind.

Stinky clay is a really smelly clay-dough. Each time you're finished playing with it, put it in something with a tight top. A coffee can will work well, or a plastic bag tied shut.

You'll need these things to make stinky clay:

A big bowl

3 tablespoons of baking powder

1/2 cup of pickle juice or vinegar

1 cup of flour

1 tablespoon of vegetable oil

X-TRA UGLY.

food coloring or poster paint (any yucky color will do)

Put the 3 tablespoons of baking powder into a bowl.

Now add 1/2 cup of pickle juice (without the pickles!) or vinegar. Don't worry, it's supposed to fizz!

Mix in 1 cup of flour and 1 tablespoon of oil. Smush the bumps with your fingers.

Last of all, add a few drops of food coloring or paint. If your mixture is too dry, add water. If it is too wet, add a little bit of flour. Mix well, until it's really stinky.

Is your clay stinky enough? Probably!

A lot of people are scared of stinky clay, but don't let this stop you from playing with it!

Face Masks

You can wear a mask anytime you want to hide your face. Some masks are scary.

Some masks are silly. My grandma even has a special mask to wear at night.

To make your mask, you need a piece of cardboard large enough to at least cover your eyes. Use your fingers to measure how far apart your eyes are. Mark this distance on your cardboard.

Hold the piece of cardboard in your hands and use scissors to make eye holes.

Can you see?

You can cut your mask . . .

in any shape.

How is your mask going to stay on? Staple a piece of string — knotted at the ends — to each side of your mask, and then tie these in the back to keep your mask on.

Use glue to add anything to your mask. All of these things make good noses.

GLUE

a button

macaroni

a cardboard tube

Hair can be made from anything too.

pipe cleaners

cut paper

yarn

socks

What else?

Don't forget to paint your mask when you're finished (but take it off first!).

Crayon Magic

Crayons smell great and are terrific for coloring and drawing.

But did you know that you can write and draw magic messages with crayons?

Using a WHITE crayon, write or draw your magic message on a WHITE piece of paper.

Give your piece of paper to a friend. If they paint the piece of paper with watercolor paint...

VOILÀ!
Your secret message will appear.

You can also trace things with crayons. To do this, you need to peel the paper off your crayon like you peel the skin off a banana.

Now find an object or a surface that is hard and bumpy.

Place your paper on top of that surface.

Rub the paper with the long side of your crayon until your tracing appears. Try tracing coins, the bottom of your shoes . . . what else?

21

You can cut out anything that you think looks interesting.

Sometimes a collage can be about an idea.

My collage is about bugs.

My collage is about the letter W.

When you're tired of cutting and tearing, you can begin to glue. You can glue your pieces onto the paper side by side . . .

or overlapping each other.

You might even want to paint or draw over your collage when you're finished.

Wow!

Hats

One of the best things about having a head is that you can easily wear hats. There are many different kinds of hats in the world. Sometimes a hat can tell you about the person who is wearing it. Can you make a hat that tells us about you?

First you need to measure around your head with a piece of string. Make a mark where the string touches itself so you know how big your head is.
Cut the string at the mark.

Now find a piece of cardboard a little longer than the piece of string. The cardboard can be as tall or short as you want it to be; really, all that matters is that it is long enough to fit around your head.

Slowly bend the cardboard by rolling it around a bottle the long way. Now your hat will fit you better.

Now glue or staple your hat together.

Put on your hat. Is it too tall? No problem — take off your hat and lay it flat again. Using scissors, cut straight across to make it shorter, or cut zigzags, waves, or bumps to make it shorter and weirder.

You can color your hat and add anything to it. Since this hat tells the world something about you, you'll know best how to decorate it!

Papier-Mâché

Papier-Mâché is another way to make sculpture. This is one of the gooiest projects we know. You'll look like this when you're finished. Wear old clothes or a smock.

Gather your materials first. You'll need:

newspapers

maybe balloons

tape

a big bowl

2 cups of flour

3 cups of water

glue

Now you're going to make the form or shape of your sculpture. This can be done by crumpling up newspaper into balls and taping them together. You can also tape balloons together to make a form.

Take the leftover newspapers and rip them into strips as wide as your arm.

Pour 2 cups of flour into the bowl. Mix in 3 cups of water and a big squirt of glue, and stir with your hands. Smush the lumps with your fingers until the goo mixture is smooth. It should be as thick as a milk shake at the end. Add more water or flour if you need to.

Dip the strips into the goo-bowl one at a time, and begin wrapping them around your form.

To make your sculpture really strong, wrap the strips in different directions. Make about three layers of strips. If it all gets too soggy, let your sculpture dry a couple of hours before continuing.

Once you've finished wrapping your form, spread a little extra goo all over the sculpture with your hand. Your sculpture will take at least a day to dry completely. Once it is dry, you can decorate it with paint, beads, or anything else you like.

Make Another You!

You're pretty amazing, so why shouldn't there be two of you? Or four?

To make another you, you'll need two really big pieces of paper. Each should be big enough so that all of you can fit on it when you lie down.

Lie down on the paper and choose your position. Can you look like you're swimming? Running? Now have a friend trace your outline with a crayon. Stay still!

If you get ticklish . . .

begin again.

Cut out your shape, and place this on the second large piece of paper.

Hold your cut-out piece with one paw and trace around its edges. Now you've drawn yourself again on the second piece of paper.

Cut yourself out again.

Put the two pieces together and start stapling around the edges.

You'll need to leave one or two holes in the sides so that you can stuff the other you with crumpled-up newspaper.

hole

hole

When you're full, staple the holes together, give yourself a hug, and decorate.

Clay Beads

Have you ever noticed what happens to clay when you forget to put it away?

It gets hard.

Hello!

Where have you been?

Here's a recipe for a kind of clay that's supposed to get hard after you shape it. Once it's hard and dry, you can paint it.

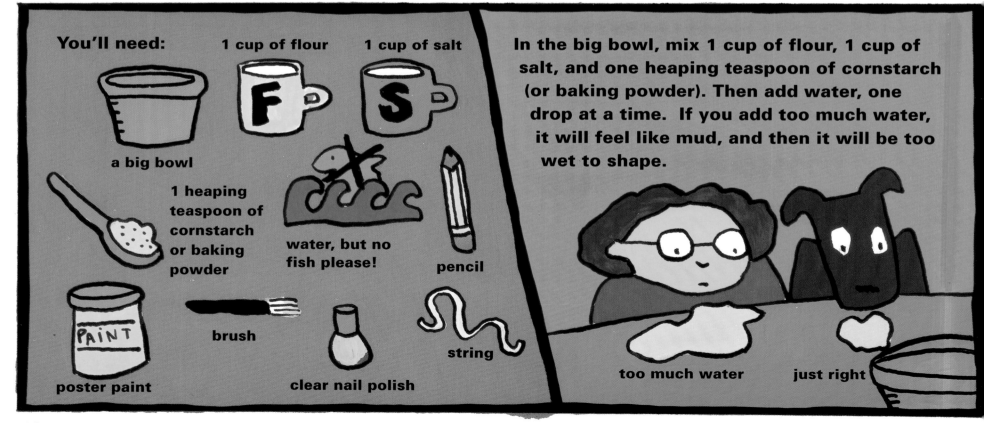

You'll need:

a big bowl

1 cup of flour

1 cup of salt

1 heaping teaspoon of cornstarch or baking powder

water, but no fish please!

pencil

poster paint

brush

clear nail polish

string

In the big bowl, mix 1 cup of flour, 1 cup of salt, and one heaping teaspoon of cornstarch (or baking powder). Then add water, one drop at a time. If you add too much water, it will feel like mud, and then it will be too wet to shape.

too much water

just right

If your clay is too wet, try adding more salt, flour, and cornstarch to make it drier. If it is too dry, add a teeny bit of water. Once the mixture feels smushy and not crumbly or gooey, you're ready to make beads.

Let's go!

To make a round bead, pinch off a piece of clay and put it in the palm of your paw. Roll it around in a circle until it becomes a ball. Now try to make a square-shaped bead or a heart-shaped bead.

Make enough beads for a necklace. Poke a hole through the center of each bead with a pencil. The hole needs to go all the way through the bead.

The beads now need time to dry. They may take up to two whole days to dry.

Go back to sleep!

We're not ready yet!

When the beads are hard and dry, you can paint them with poster paint. Make sure the paint doesn't block the bead's hole. To be extra fancy, paint your beads with clear nail polish once the poster paint has dried. This will make them shiny.

String your beads and wear them out to dinner. People will be amazed by how beautiful they are!

33

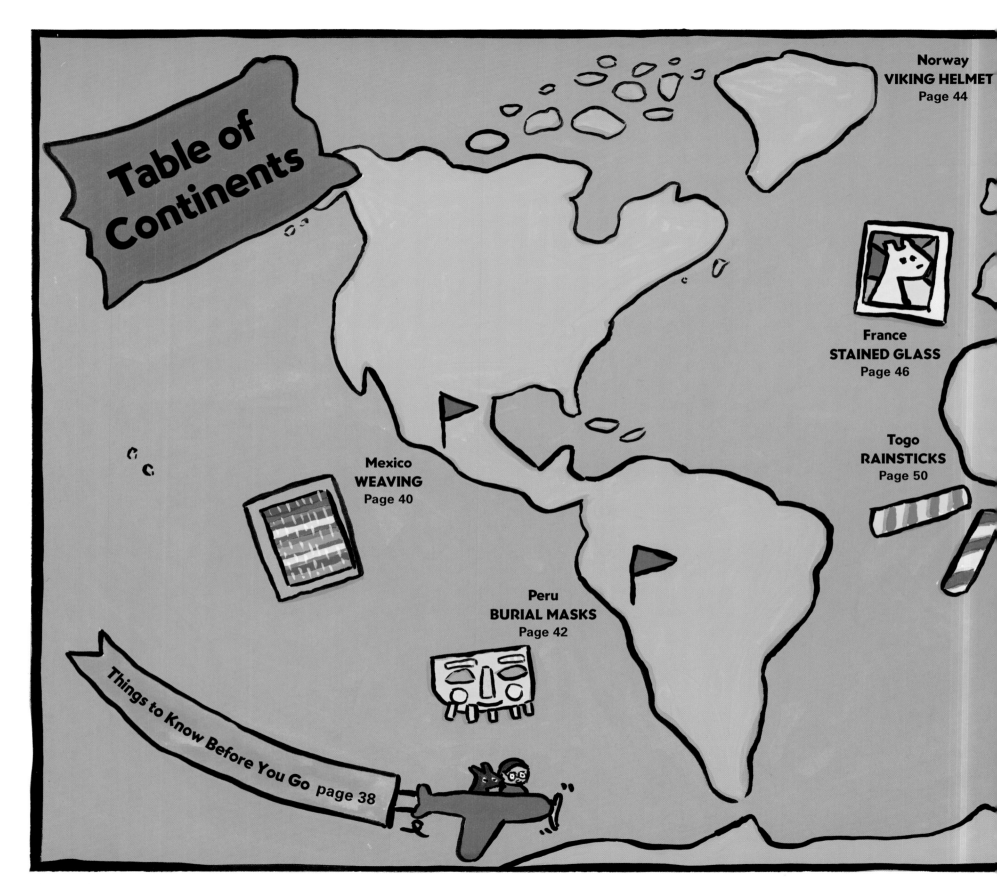

Table of Continents

Italy
MOSAICS
Page 48

China
SCROLLS
Page 60

Egypt
PAPER
Page 52

India
BLOCK PRINTS
Page 54

Bali
SHADOW PUPPETS
Page 58

Java
BATIK
Page 56

GOODBYE
Page 62

Things to Know Before You Go

After you choose which country you want to visit, read through the whole project before you start. This way, you'll know what materials you need. For the BATIK and PAPER projects you will need an adult along—make sure they're around *before* you begin.

If a project sounds goopy or uses paint, work on newspaper! (You may want to wear a big T-shirt or old clothes so *you* don't get gooped.)

You can cut up boxes to get cardboard. Some cardboard, like shirt cardboard and cereal box cardboard, is thinner and easier to cut. If it seems too floppy, glue two pieces together.

For this book you'll only ever need white glue. If the glue dries on your hands (or paws), rub them together—it peels right off.

thick

thin

thin

We love masking tape—it's the only kind of tape we used on our trip around the world. We found it to be very handy.

We almost always use poster paint, which is sometimes called tempera paint. You can mix any color in the world using poster paint. Cleanup is easier if you mix small amounts in paper cups, plastic cups, or egg cartons. Just throw the leftover paint away!

Don't forget to clean up when you finish a project. Wash your paintbrushes *before* the paint dries on them. Shake dry!

Art is an adventure. Adventures are fun because they are full of surprises. Art can be surprising, too. Remember, there is no right or wrong way your art should look when it is finished.

Weaving
Mexico

Look down at yourself. Your clothing is made of many, many different pieces of thread. One way of putting threads together to make cloth is called *weaving*.

Today I weave, yesterday I wove.

What did you do the day before?

I don't see anything.

In Mexico many people weave by hand. These woven pieces of cloth are useful and decorative. Art can be found in unusual places.

There goes more art!

All weaving is done on looms. To make a loom, cut 4 strips of cardboard as long as this book. Glue these pieces together in a square.

Cut small slits a finger-space apart on the outside of the top of the loom. Now do the same on the opposite bottom edge.

Go get a really long piece of string. Tape one end to the loom's top corner and slip the string into the first slit. Wrap the string around the loom using every slit. When you're finished, cut off any extra string and tape the end to the cardboard. These up and down strings are called *warp*.

Weft is the word for whatever you weave with. Weft can be:

ribbons

yarn

old fabric

old socks

heavy string

What about weft?

What?

Begin at the top of the loom and weave across. If you are using a thin weft, tie one end to the warp. You can go over and under the warp strings like this:

or around them like this:

We wrapped the warp, and wove the weft. We're almost finished weaving, since there's no weft left!

Leave your weaving on the loom when you are finished and hang it up, or undo the weaving and start again!

41

Burial Masks
Peru

Here we are in Peru, where archaeologists have discovered a mummy hundreds of years old. The mummy is wearing a mask and is buried with bowls, pots, and clothing.

Gee, that's a lot of stuff.

Ancient Peruvians believed that they would go on to another life after they died. All of the things buried with the mummy were for his next life.

The mummy's mask is made of gold and gems; someone worked hard to make it. We can tell that the mummy was an important and rich person because his mask is so elaborate.

You can make your own mask that will show how important you are. Find or excavate:

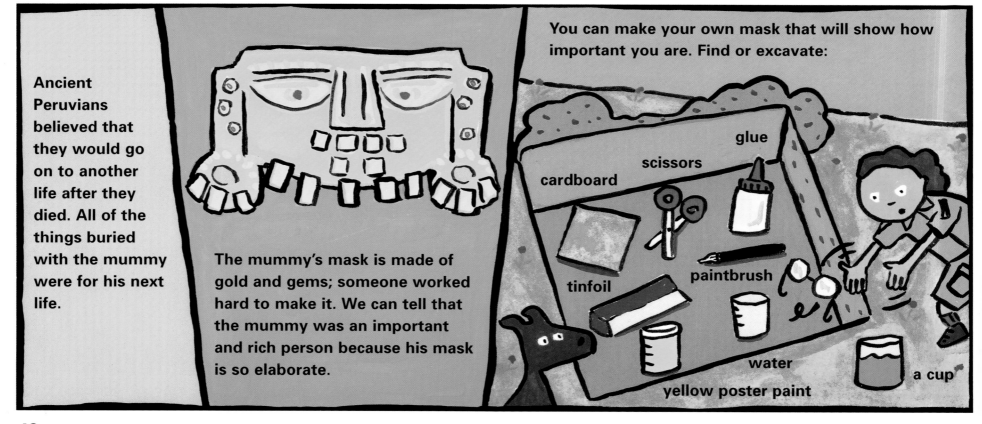

glue

scissors

cardboard

paintbrush

tinfoil

water

yellow poster paint

a cup

Cut a piece of cardboard in a shape like this:

To make eyeholes, carefully poke through the mask with the point of the scissors and then cut around.

Look in a mirror. What shapes are your nose, mouth, ears, and eyebrows? Cut out pieces of cardboard to make these shapes and glue them onto your mask. If you're using thin cardboard, you can glue pieces on top of each other to make more detail.

Cover the front of the mask with glue. Lay a piece of tinfoil on top and gently smooth it over the raised pieces. Fold the edges of the tinfoil over onto the back and glue them. Poke out the eyes with your finger.

In a cup, mix two big squirts of glue and two big squirts of yellow paint. Dip your brush in water before you start painting. After you've painted the mask, try drawing designs into the wet paint with the opposite end of the brush.

When the paint dries, tape a pencil to the back of your mask and hold the mask up to your face.

I didn't know mummies wore glasses!

Viking Helmets Norway

We are on our way to Norway to visit the Vikings who lived there more than one thousand years ago. The Vikings sailed all over the world in boats like this one.

When there was no wind, they rowed!

Fjord Explorer

The Vikings invaded and conquered many countries. When they fought battles, they wore metal helmets that they made themselves.

Agh! I left my helmet in England!

The Vikings made other useful things that were beautiful too.

swords

brooches

coins

Here is a way you can make a Viking helmet. Look around your house and plunder:

a balloon

a big bowl

1 cup of flour

1 and 1/2 cups of water

gloo

glue

newspaper ripped into short strips

scissors

cardboard

poster paint

paintbrush

Blow up the balloon until it is a little bit bigger than your head. Are you ready to papier-mâché? In the bowl, mix the flour and the water with a squirt of glue. Battle the lumps.

Dip the strips of newspaper into the papier-mâché and cover the top half of the balloon. Keep adding strips until the helmet is pretty thick.

That's swell, Sven!

In a day, when your helmet seems dry, pop the balloon to let the inside dry too. If you put your helmet in a sunny place, it will dry faster.

Viking helmets usually had nose guards to protect noses. Cut a piece of cardboard and glue it to the front of your helmet.

Paint your helmet and have fun with your next invasion!

Stained Glass France

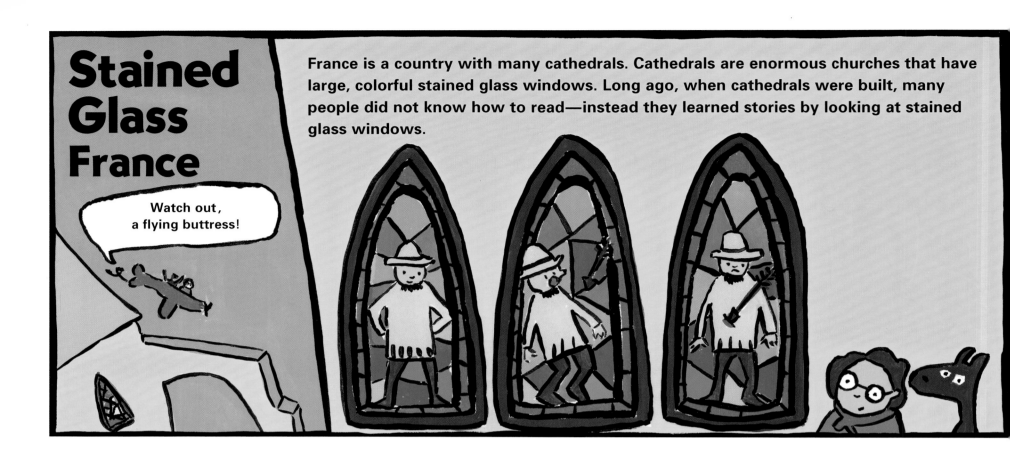

Watch out, a flying buttress!

France is a country with many cathedrals. Cathedrals are enormous churches that have large, colorful stained glass windows. Long ago, when cathedrals were built, many people did not know how to read—instead they learned stories by looking at stained glass windows.

In a stained glass window, every color is a different piece of glass. Black lead holds the pieces together.

I feel so blue.

Here's a way for you to make stained glass using plastic wrap. You'll need:

a piece of plastic wrap

a piece of white paper

tape

glue

black poster paint

other colors of poster paint

paper cups

paintbrushes

a piece of wax paper

You're going to paint on the plastic wrap. Lay it flat on the white paper and tape down the edges.

Put a small amount of paint into each cup, then squirt in an equal amount of glue. Mix together well.

The black paint–glue mixture will look like the lead. Use it to paint the outlines of your picture.

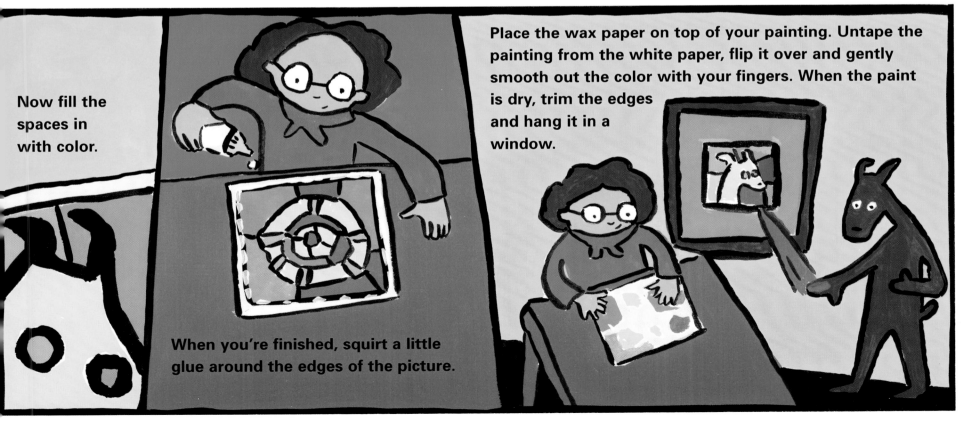

Now fill the spaces in with color.

When you're finished, squirt a little glue around the edges of the picture.

Place the wax paper on top of your painting. Untape the painting from the white paper, flip it over and gently smooth out the color with your fingers. When the paint is dry, trim the edges and hang it in a window.

Mosaics
Italy

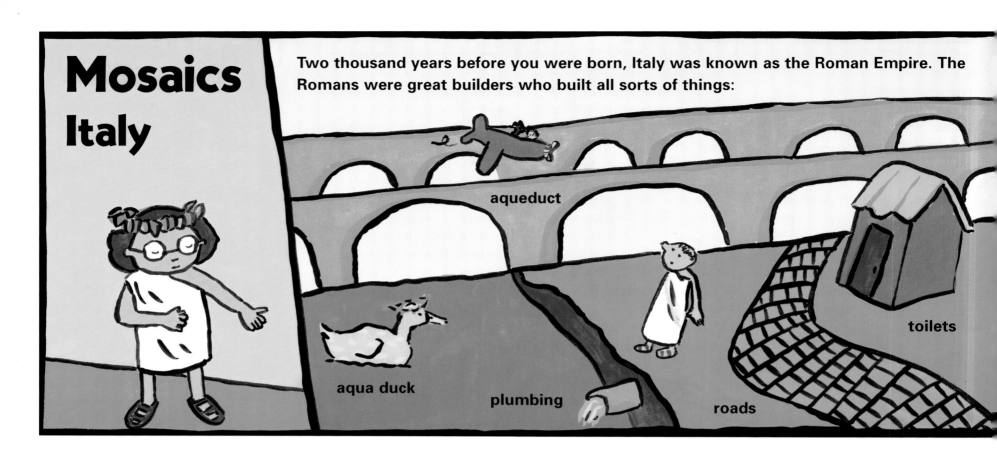

Two thousand years before you were born, Italy was known as the Roman Empire. The Romans were great builders who built all sorts of things:

aqueduct

aqua duck

plumbing

roads

toilets

In Roman homes, mosaics were popular. A mosaic is a floor or wall decoration made with many small pieces of colored tile.

Oops!

Together the small pieces make up a bigger picture or design.

STUCKUS DOG US

First find . . .

scissors

lots of cardboard

poster paint—many colors

Now you're ready to make tiles. Cut the cardboard into strips as wide as your toes.

Is this why we're wearing sandals?

Paint each strip a different color. When the paint dries, cut the strips into squares.

Now roam around and get:

brown poster paint

glue

a cup

and a shallow container like:

a Styrofoam tray

a shoebox lid

a pie tin

a paper or plastic plate

Fill the cup a quarter of the way with the brown paint. Now add glue until the cup is halfway full. Mix well and pour into your container.

Push the tiles gently into the mixture to make your mosaic. Use one color of tile to make the outline of a picture. Then fill in with the other colors.

Quackus.

Rainsticks
Togo

To Togo we go-go!

Throughout Africa, many kinds of instruments are played. Instruments like these are used in traditional ceremonies and celebrations:

rattle

harp

long drum

slit drum

xylophone

Here we are in Togo, listening to rainsticks. The rainstick is an unusual instrument that makes a sound like falling rain when it is slowly turned upside down. Rainsticks like these are also found in South America.

To make a rainstick you need:

a paper towel tube

two handfuls of uncooked rice

glue

heavy paper

masking tape and . . .

about 23 nails slightly shorter than the width of the tube.

Starting at the top of the tube, poke the nails through the tube in a spiral.

The tube will look like this from the side . . .

and top.

Tape a piece of paper to cover one end of the rainstick. Pour in the rice.

Cover and tape the other end shut.

Now wrap the entire rainstick with masking tape.

Glue paper onto the outside of the rainstick. Now you can draw or paint on it. Other good decorations are yarn, ribbons, glitter . . .

Paper
Egypt

Here we are in Egypt, where some of the first artists invented paper so they would have something permanent to draw and write on. The Egyptians made their paper from a plant called papyrus. These days, paper is made from wood and recycled paper.

Whew! The cats here are big!

Paper, papyrus—those words sound alike.

We know a lot about the Egyptians because they wrote down everything they did on scrolls of papyrus.

Dear Diary, Today I invented paper. Then I had lunch . . .

Here's a way you can make paper. Go get:

newspaper

colored paper or craft tissue

water

two big bowls

a blender

two pieces of screen the size of your face

a sponge

an adult

First tear some of the newspaper into small pieces. Tear up the colored paper too. Put the pieces in the bowl, cover with water, and soak for a couple of hours.

I'm disintegrating, decomposing, dissolving, and deteriorating.

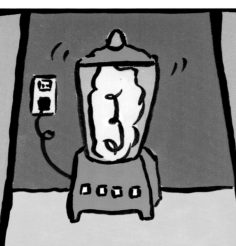

Get your adult and pour some of the soaked paper and water into the blender. Blend to a pulp. Add water if the pulp clumps up. Let your adult have a turn too.

Put the screen on a thick layer of newspaper. Glop the pulp onto the screen and spread it out evenly. You can place flat things like stickers, leaves, flowers, and glitter on top of the pulp. Now put the other screen on top.

Take the sponge and press down hard on the pulp through the screen. Squeeze the water out of the sponge into the empty bowl. Press and squeeze again. Change the newspaper layer when it gets wet.

When no more water comes out of the pulp, gently peel the top screen away. Lay the *paper* on fresh newspaper to dry. It will take a couple of days. In the meantime, try these neat-o Egyptian poses!

Block Prints India

Many different kinds of things in the world are printed. Newspapers are, and so was this book. Block printing is one of the oldest and simplest ways to print. Here in India, wood blocks are used to print on fabric.

The wood blocks take many months to carve. Everything is carved away except for the design, which sticks out of the block in a relief.

I'm finally finished.

That's a relief!

Here's another way to make a printing block. You'll need:

a Styrofoam meat tray (wash it off with soap)

scissors

glue

a small piece of cardboard

a snack

a pencil

tape

a stamp pad

INK

paper

54

Cut out a flat piece of tray no bigger than the stamp pad. Glue it to the cardboard and then trim the edges. This is your printing block.

Eat your snack and let the glue dry!

block head

The design you'll carve into your block can be a picture, letters, or just squiggles and dots. If the design goes to the edge, you will be able to connect your prints.

Ready? Use the pencil to draw *into* the Styrofoam. Trace over it again so the design is really pushed into the Styrofoam.

Make a handle for the block back with a piece of folded-over tape.

Now print! Press the printing block firmly onto the stamp pad and then onto the paper.

Batik

Java

Here in Java people wear beautiful batik cloth. In Java, batik is made by drawing designs on cloth with wax. When the cloth is dyed different colors, the design stays the original color because the wax protects it by resisting the dye.

Some batik designs use familiar shapes and others have more abstract shapes and patterns.

Here's what you'll need to make batik:

a piece of an old white cotton sheet

tape

an adult with an iron

a white candle

newspaper

watercolor paint

Pressing down hard with the *unlit* candle, draw your design on the sheet.

Tape the sheet piece to a table. Stretch it flat and tight as you tape. Now it will be easier to draw on.

Untape the sheet and place it between a couple of layers of newspaper. Have your adult carefully iron the newspaper.

Watch your fingers!

Now, using watercolor paint, paint the sheet different colors. Put it on a new piece of newspaper to dry. When it has dried, you can batik a second time if you want. Draw new designs, iron, and paint over the whole thing again!

HOT JAVA DAILY NEWS

The iron melts the wax into the cotton. The newspaper blots the extra wax. You'll only have to iron for a minute or so.

Shadow Puppets
Bali

Have you ever told a story with art? Of course you have. You do this every time you paint or draw a picture. Another way you can use art to tell a story is with puppets. Here we are in Bali, watching shadow puppets.

The puppet master, who is called a *dalang*, sits behind a cloth screen with his puppets. The audience sits on the other side and sees only the puppets' shadows.

It's almost like going to the movies!

Bali button

Shadow puppets are flat but have many small holes. The holes make the puppets' shadows look more interesting.

Go get:

thin cardboard

scissors

a hole puncher

tape

a few pencils or chopsticks

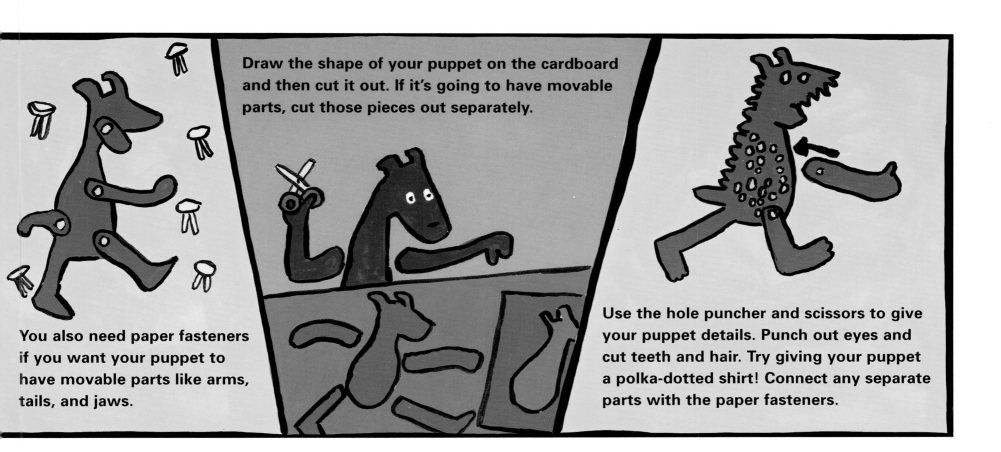

You also need paper fasteners if you want your puppet to have movable parts like arms, tails, and jaws.

Draw the shape of your puppet on the cardboard and then cut it out. If it's going to have movable parts, cut those pieces out separately.

Use the hole puncher and scissors to give your puppet details. Punch out eyes and cut teeth and hair. Try giving your puppet a polka-dotted shirt! Connect any separate parts with the paper fasteners.

You need a way to hold and move your shadow puppet. Tape two pencils or chopsticks together and then tape one end to the puppet's body. Tape pencils or chopsticks to the movable parts as well.

In a dark room, hang a sheet across a doorway.

Put a light behind the sheet and then, sit behind the light. Your audience will be able to see the shadows best if your puppets are close to the sheet. Use one hand to hold the puppet and the other to move the different parts.

Scrolls
China

Stand still, shut your eyes, and turn your head all the way to the left. Now open your eyes and turn your head all the way to the right. The big view you see is called a panorama. Can a panorama fit into a painting?

Panda!

Possibly.

Perhaps.

Perfectly.

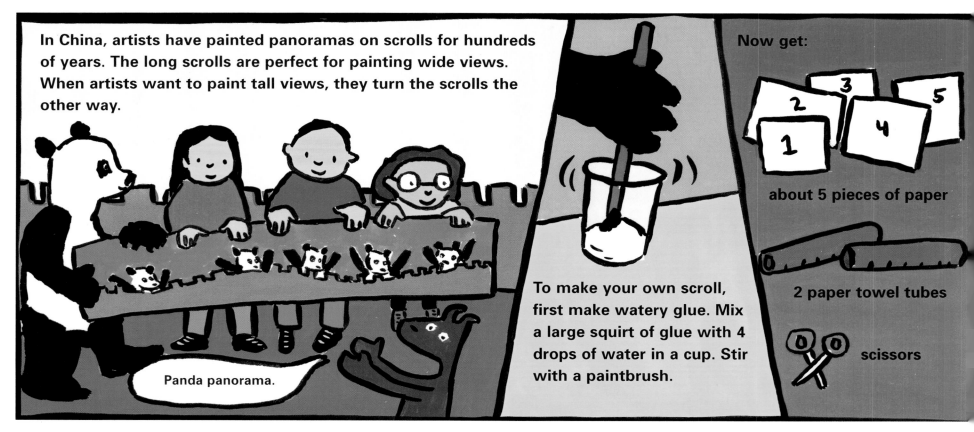

In China, artists have painted panoramas on scrolls for hundreds of years. The long scrolls are perfect for painting wide views. When artists want to paint tall views, they turn the scrolls the other way.

Panda panorama.

To make your own scroll, first make watery glue. Mix a large squirt of glue with 4 drops of water in a cup. Stir with a paintbrush.

Now get:

about 5 pieces of paper

2 paper towel tubes

scissors

If the paper is taller than the tubes, trim it down until it is the same size.

Lay all the paper end to end, slightly overlapping the edges. Glue the edges together with the watery glue so that you have one long piece of paper.

Panda pandemonium.

Ready to scroll? Smear one tube with glue and wrap the end of the paper around it. Hold with both hands until the glue sticks. Glue the second tube to the other end of the paper scroll.

Now you're ready to paint. Add 3 drops of water to any paint you use. This makes it thinner so it will not crack when you roll the scroll.

Try painting with these things:

yarn taped on a pencil

a comb

a pencil eraser

a feather

steel wool

someone's tail

When your painted panorama dries, roll it up. Take your scroll with you wherever you go, and remember to always look for the big view.

We hope you enjoyed your trip with us. Keep your eyes open for all the different kinds of art in *your* part of the world, and come traveling again with us soon!

Loo-Loo and **Boo** first rose to fame on the nationally acclaimed television series *Art 'Til Ya Drop!* Boo is a graduate of the world-renowned Beaux Arts Des Chiens, and Loo-Loo has just begun second grade at the prestigious L.M.N. Tary School in New York City. They met Denis Mary Roche, a former teacher, at the annual Stinky Clay Free-Throw Competition.